FROM THE ROMANS TO B&Q

A History of Wyberton

Edited by Richard and Alison Austin

Wyberton History Group

Published by Wyberton History Group,
Cherry Tree Cottage, Low Road, Wyberton,
Boston, Lincolnshire PE21 7AP

Copyright © Richard and Alison Austin 1999

ISBN 0 9536875 0 3

No part of this book may be reproduced, stored in a retrieval system or transmitted in any form,
or by any means electronic, mechanical, photocopying, recording or otherwise
without the prior permission of the Publisher and the Copyright holders.

Printed in Great Britain by Richaprint Ltd.,
Priory Road, Freiston, Boston, Lincolnshire.

Contents

Parish Map	Pages 2-3
Foreword	4
Introduction	5

Early Days

Roman Wyberton	8
Domesday	11
Wybert	12
Wybert's Castle	12

Religion

Christianity	16
St. Leodegar's Church	17
St. Leodegar	20
List of Rectors	21
The United Reformed Church	22
Methodist Chapels	22

Farming

Medieval Map	24
Agriculture	26
Mechanisation of Wyberton Farms	32
Hemp	36
Woad	36
Milk in the Twentieth Century	38
Killing the Pig	41

The Community

Parish Affairs	44
Education	52
Sugar Rents	55
Wyberton Mills	56
Blacksmith's Shops and Forges	58
Brickmaking	62

River and Marsh

Rennie's Map of the Haven	66-67
The Straightening of the Haven	68
Lighting the Navigation Lamps	78
Floods and Drainage	79
Wildfowling	82
A Day out on Wyberton Marsh	84
The Marsh Reserves	86

People and Places

Ralphs Lane Gibbet	90
The Murder of a Policeman	91
The Hammer and Pincers	93
The Pincushion and the Pinfold	94
Wyberton Park	96
Tytton Hall	98
Janet Elizabeth Lane-Claypon	99
Fred Parkes	100
E.W. Bowser	101
Dickie Dale	102
Wyberton Airfield	104

Communications

Roads and Lanes	108
First Telephones	110
Fuel	111
Wyberton's Two Railways	112

Wars

The Civil War	116
World War One	116
The Second World War	119
Brigadier General R.L. Aldecron	121

Wyberton Past and Present

Memories	124
Shopping in 1999	125
Wyberton's Industries	126
Wyberton Clubs and Societies	128
Road Names	131

Acknowledgements	133
Wyberton History Group	134

THE PARISH OF WYBERTON (AREA IN WHITE)

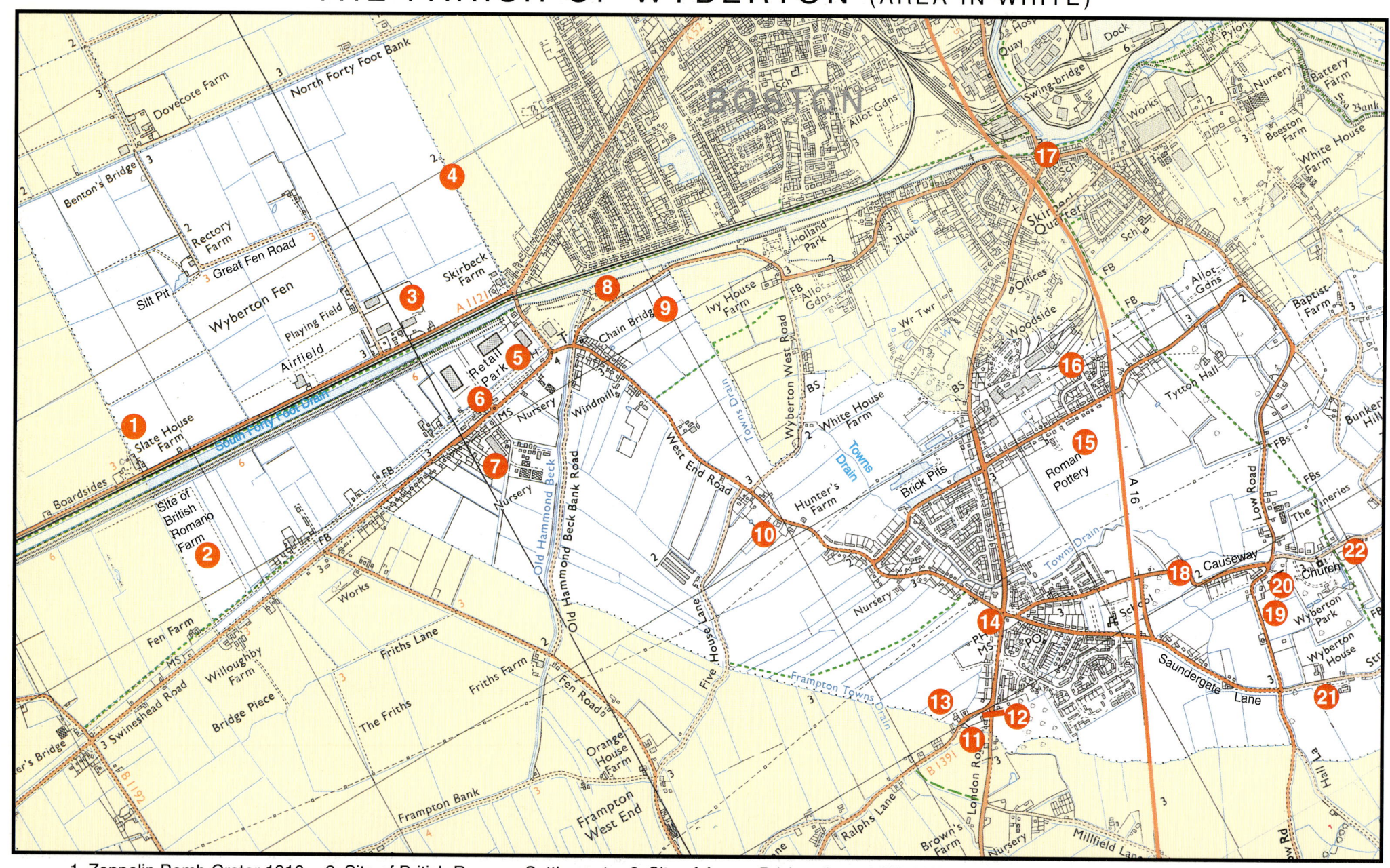

1. Zeppelin Bomb Crater 1916   2. Site of British Romano Settlement   3. Site of Armes Brickworks   4. World War 2 Auxilliary Hideout   5. Hammer and Pincers
6. Site of the parish Workhouse   7. Mastenbroeks   8. Chain Bridge Pumping Station   9. Roman Pottery Found   10. Old Methodist Chapel   11. Site of Ralph's Gibbet
12. Blaclsmiths Shop   13. Site of Methodist School   14. Pincushion and site of Pinfold   15. Roman Pottery   16. Calders   17. Site of Tollbar   18. Galley's Corner
19. Old School   20. Roman Pottery   21. Site of Woad Mill   22. Policeman shot here

THE PARISH OF WYBERTON (AREA IN WHITE)

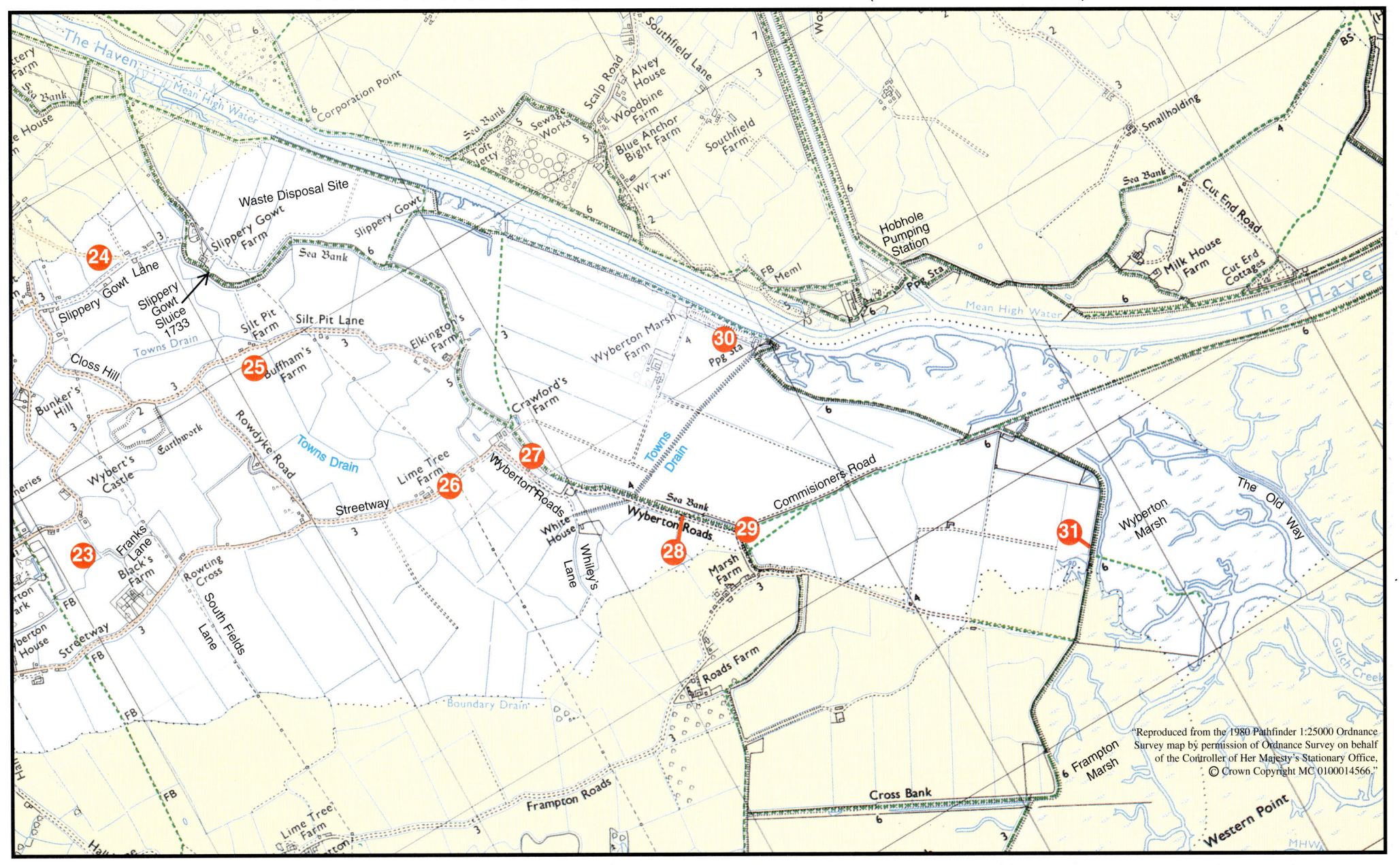

23. Site of Medieval Windmill 24. Red Rose 25. Site of Silt Pit 26. Old Methodist Chapel 27 World War 2 Pillbox 28. Derelict Ship Inn 29. World War 2 Pillbox
30. Wyberton Marsh Pumping Station 31. Site of J. Colam's Hut

Foreword
by Councillor Alan Day DFC JP, Mayor of Boston 1998-9

The parish of Wyberton has been my home for the past 50 years, in four different dwellings but never more than a mile from St. Leodegar's. During that time I have accumulated some knowledge of the area, from the marsh to the mill. I am therefore pleased to write a preface to a production that has exceeded all expectations.

From the beginning of the project there has been considerable interest and the content of the book reflects the diversity of that interest. Some of the articles are lengthy, some virtually one liners, but all are relevant to the village.

Help has come from a wide range of people, with historical as well as current local knowledge, and all directed and collected by Alison and Richard Austin.

Financial help was needed and was willingly given by B&Q, Awards for All and The Borough of Boston. The result is a book of which we should all be proud and is a tribute to a village with deep historical roots and a vibrant future.

May I congratulate all concerned and wish 'Romans to B&Q' every success.

Alan Day
Wyberton

Introduction

by Richard and Alison Austin

In 1998 Wyberton History Group was formed to research, record and preserve the history of the Parish and to write this book as a Millennium project. The aim is to enlighten present and future inhabitants of their heritage. It is also thought that the 4000 residents may like to have a greater understanding of the history that has created their surroundings. Finally there is the hope that this study of the development of a village community, over a two thousand year period, will interest a wider audience.

Wyberton is a long and narrow parish lying to the south and west of Boston. It is six miles long and less than a mile wide; a typical shape of parishes adjacent to the Wash. It stretches from the sea marsh along the Haven, to Chain Bridge and a further mile to the North Forty Foot Drain beyond the Rugby Club. Newcomers may be surprised to learn that St. Leodegar's Parish Church is geographically in the centre of Wyberton. They may be equally surprised to know of the wealth of features there are within the Parish boundaries.

The first evidence of human occupation dates back to the Romans. The earliest tentative written records are some one thousand years later in the Norman period but it is the sixteenth century, in the reign of Henry VIII, before there is any volume of records.

The sea marsh, the Haven estuary and the fresh water fen at the other end of the Parish over time have had a big influence on this low lying land. They have dictated the need for the sea banks, the course of the drainage channels and to a large extent the layout of the road system. From the Victorian era onwards the construction of the two major Turnpike routes along what are now the London and Swineshead Roads have also greatly influenced the development of the village as it is today.

Until the end of the 19th century the story of Wyberton is one of a very close, self-sufficient and independent community. This century has seen great change which accelerated after the Second World War with the building of a large number of houses centred round London Road. More recently, the construction of the out of town retail park at Chain Bridge has again heralded a transformation and brought with it Wyberton's latest arrival, B&Q.

The Wyberton story is one of achievement and change punctuated by disasters and tragedies. The rediscovery of so many unrecorded events and things long forgotten makes a fascinating study.

200-year old Turkey Oak in Church Lane in winter

Early Days

Roman Wyberton by S. Membery, J. and W. Parker

The people who lived in Roman Wyberton were probably farmers, salt producers and fishermen. There is evidence from broken pottery dating from the first and second centuries and some marks in a field. Broken sherds of Roman pots have been found at four sites within the parish, two of which indicate settlement.

Roman field system

The pottery finds near the A16 Trunk Road and at Chain Bridge possibly indicate these to be sites where salt was made. Salt was a valuable commodity in the Roman period and was a prime reason for settlement in the Fenland. It was produced by evaporating saline water in shallow pans over a fire. At this period it is thought that these parts of Wyberton could have been on the edge of The Haven.

'Soil marks' on an aerial photograph taken in 1964 revealed the site of British-Romano farming. The field concerned is to the south of the South Forty Foot Drain and butts up to the Frampton boundary. These marks appeared after the field had been deep ploughed. An investigation showed they had been caused by filled-in drainage ditches which had been dug by farmers in the first or second centuries to drain their fields. The shapes are typical and pottery of the Roman period was found in association with them.

The other site where pottery has been found, near the old school at the junction of Causeway with the Low Road, simply represents a stray find.

Much of the pottery from the parish is grey ware or colour coated from the Nene Valley but Samian ware, a high class type of pottery from central and southern Gaul, has also been recovered. Other pottery includes vessels of the Mortaria type for food preparation as well as other domestic pots. It is known from excavations in Boston Borough that pottery known as Black Burnished Ware from Dorset was brought here and it is highly likely that examples of this lie, yet to be discovered, in Wyberton. Also found in the parish are strange ball-like objects composed of fired clay. These have also been found on excavated sites in nearby parishes and, as yet, no one has been able to explain their function.

Wyberton was in contact with the wider Roman world through trade links. Most long distance trade at this time was carried by boats which coastal hopped, bringing goods from Dorset and the Humber region. The many inland watercourses converging on Wyberton would have also been utilised, with goods being traded with Lincoln to the north and the Midlands to the West. Although the exact nature of the boats is not known, a model recovered from Fishbourne Palace can give us an idea of the form of one type of large Roman ship. These boats transported a wide range of goods including grain, wine and other foodstuffs, often contained in large pots known as amphorae, and they also traded ceramics. The Haven at Wyberton would have been a safe anchorage.

Tacitus, the Roman author, helps us to envisage the ships which may have been seen in The Haven during the three hundred years of Roman occupation:

Some were shallow draft, pointed at bow and stern to withstand heavy seas, others were flat bottomed to facilitate grounding. Most were equipped with steering oars at both ends for quick forward and backward movement and to make them easy to manoeuvre in restricted waters. The merchant ships were designed to carry as much cargo as possible and were known as 'round' ships. These ships had beams of approximately one third their length and were usually between 250 and 500 tonnes. With the odd exception, they were propelled entirely by sail at sea. A boat was often towed behind to act as a harbour tug when required.

Both the warships and the merchantmen had figureheads on or near the bow and the sterns were also decorated. Merchant ships usually bore the insignia of a basket placed above the stern. River cargo boats were long and curved at both ends.

It is clear that the occupation in Wyberton was relatively modest as no villas or other indications of wealth are evident, but this is typical of the fenland, which was nevertheless well populated. It was presumably controlled from elsewhere in the higher hinterland. It could be that the output of salt was not enough to sustain a wealthy economy or perhaps intermittent flooding was a problem.

Postscript: 18th and 19th century authors were convinced that the sea bank and some of the drainage was the work of the Romans but there is no archeological evidence to support these theories. There is plenty to show that the banks were begun in the early Middle Ages.

Model of Roman ship recovered from Fishbourne Palace, Sussex

Brent Geese over the Marsh

Wyberton at Domesday by Betty Coy

After his victory at the battle of Hastings in October 1066, William the Conqueror set about reorganizing his new English Kingdom. English landowners were displaced and their lands divided between his loyal supporters.

King William ordered that a survey should be made of his new kingdom to record the approximate area of each parish, who held the land, the type of population, number of churches and most important of all how much tax or 'geld' was due. Also recorded was the owner and value in the time of King Edward. This work was completed in 1086 and became known as the 'Domesday Book'. It names Earl Edwin of Mercia as the Saxon former owner of Wyberton.

In Lincolnshire the chief recipient of land was Alan Rufus, Earl of Brittany and Richmond otherwise known as Count Alan. He is reputed to have played a prominent part in the Battle of Hastings. He was given 450 Manors which formerly belonged to Edwin, including Wyberton. About half of these Manors were in Lincolnshire, the rest being scattered throughout England. He then built himself an impressive castle at Richmond in Yorkshire from which he administered his estates. The other land owner in the parish was Guy of Craon.

The Domesday Book indicates that Wyberton must have been a fairly productive parish. Count Alan is recorded to have *a church, 12 acres of meadow, 34 sokemen (free peasants) land for 36 ½ teams of oxen plus nine carucates and 13 bovates of land. There is also a note that Edelric held it and it was worth 20 shillings.* Guy of Craon is recorded as having *10 acres of meadow, eleven bovates of land occupied by Adestan and land for 14 ½ oxen. He is said to have had two teams of oxen, two bordars (lowly ranked villeins) and in 1066 it was worth 60 shillings now 50 shillings.* A carucate is usually thought to be about 160 acres and a bovate 20 acres. However Domesday scholars warn against taking these areas too literally, they suggest it is more a measure of tax due rather than a precise area of the parish. In 1086 Lincolnshire was one of the most prosperous areas of the country and therefore highly taxed. Within the County, Holland and Kesteven were more highly taxed than Lindsey and within the local area Wyberton seems to be more highly taxed than some of its neighbours with much better, lighter soil!

In this survey of Wyberton there is no mention of salt pans for the production from sea water of this then valuable commodity. Frampton, by contrast, is recorded to have 15 salt pans. The process requires a sheltered shore regularly covered by high tides and ample supplies of light silt soil. This lack of salt pans in Wyberton indicates that the silt on the marsh was heavy, then as now. There is positive evidence of only one salt pan in the parish in an area now buried under the refuse dump shown on the map on page 24. Until recently this land was farmed by Colin Brotherton who recalls the soil of the 'hill' and surrounding field as being light silt.

The scholars also point out that the 'sokeman' or free peasants as a class inherited their independence from the Danish settlers two hundred years previously. The fact that mainly sokemen are listed in Wyberton probably reflects that the parish was populated by ancestors of men of the Danish army.

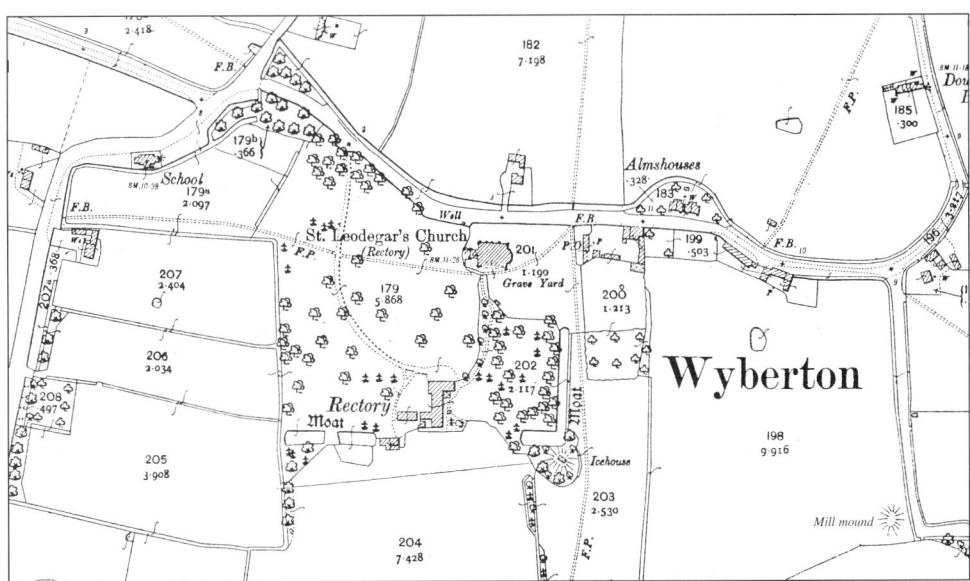

Church Lane area, 1887

The Legend of Wybert by Hilary Healey

Wyberton is named after a man called Wybert, just as Algarkirk is named after Algar. However the legend of a battle between the Danes and three Christian Saxon earls or kings was invented by a monk called Ingulph, from Crowland Abbey. He described vividly a battle against the Danes fought by the earls Algar, Morcar and Wybert at a place called Laundon. Later the battle site was identified as Threekingham, on the grounds that the name meant 'Three King Ham'. However this idea was misconstrued. The splendid saga was part of an elaborate fraud to establish credentials to land ownership.

As to Wybert's Castle, this seems to be a very modern invention, as it does not appear in any references until the first big scale Ordnance Survey maps of 1887. Whoever dreamed up this idea remains the biggest mystery. So the truth is less romantic. There was a Wybert after whom the village is named, but he had no castle and we are unlikely ever to know anything more about him.

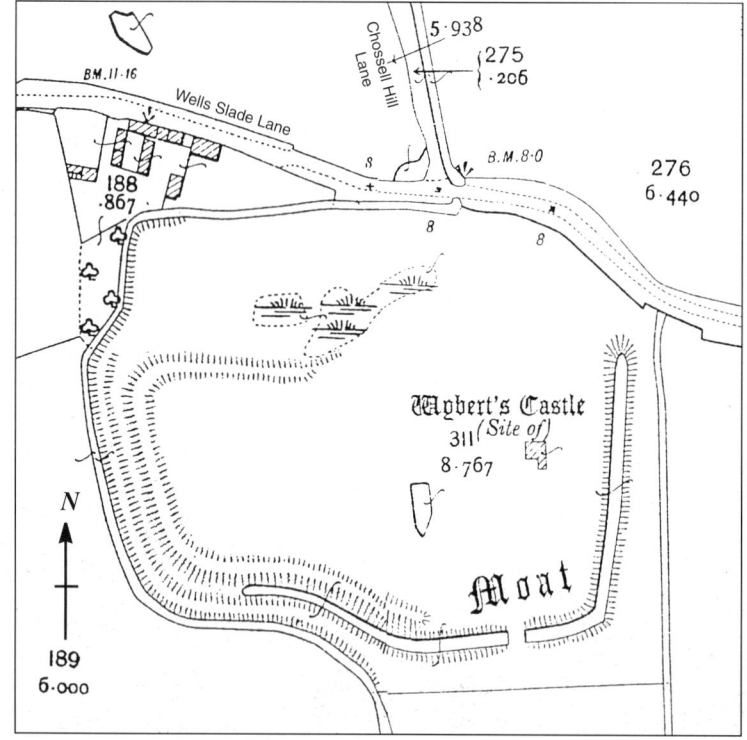

Map of the site of Wybert's Castle, 1903

Wybert's Castle by Hilary Healey

Wybert's Castle is the impressive moated site half a mile east of the church. This name is quite modern, evidently inspired by the fictitious account of Saxon battles written by one Ingulph, a medieval monk at Crowland. The biggest mystery may be, who decided to call this earthwork Wybert's Castle?

The earliest records of this site name it as Wells Slade in 1541. 'Slade' was a local name for the channel of a watercourse - in Northants and Cambridgeshire it means a valley, but this is not appropriate in the fens. There were only two major landowners in Wyberton at the time of the Domesday Book (1086), one based at Tytton (now Tytton Hall), the other almost certainly at Wells Slade. Much of the parish was held by 'sokemen', tenants of the manorial lords, who had certain privileges. The Wells were a prominent family in the 14th century who held a manor in Wyberton, identified as this site. Formerly it had been part of the Domesday lands of Count Alan of Brittany. Pieces of pottery as early as the 12th century were dug up here in 1960, together with fragmentary stone foundations and pieces of medieval glazed roof tile. These items were too slight to determine whether from houses or barns, but stone in the fens implies some status.

Adam de Wells died in 1310, his estate being left to three sons, all under age. The family owned land all over the country as well as in Wyberton, so clearly were quite prosperous and may not have been living here for very long. The inventory taken at the death of wealthy owner William Leysse in 1541 suggests a substantial house although, unusually, individual rooms and buildings are not named. The house on this site seems to have been disused by the 17th century.

The earthwork covers nearly four hectares, and consits of high ground (for the Fens) surrounded by a substantial moat. In the past there would have been more water in it than there is today, supplied by channelling the Towns Drain along the 'slade' and out to the sea. Many aerial pictures have been taken which reveal various features. The photograph suggests a causeway coming in from Chossell Hill Lane from the north. The moats on the other three sides are clearly visible as well as a shallow ditch part way across the centre of the site. To the bottom right of the site are rectangular hollows, possibly formal garden or fish ponds.

Formal garden ponds would belong with a house of the 15th or 16th century. This is about the same time as William Leysse was living here. On the left hand side of the site the uneven ground suggests buried foundations and this is where stone foundations were found in 1960.

The building shown in the photograph of the 'dig' was merely a temporary stock shelter. The building shown on the site on the 1903 map had vanished and has not been identified. The farm buildings outside the moated area to the northwest survived in part until the 1960's.

The site has been pasture for many years and is believed to have the additional interest of a good range of wild plant species. A more modern local name for the site is 'Klondyke', on account of the number of people who have imagined treasure there. The site's historical importance has been recognized and it is a Scheduled Ancient Monument, but it is not open to the public.

Excavation in 1960 by the Boston Archaeology Group

Aerial photograph 1996 taken from the North-east

Church Lane in 1947

Religion

Christianity in Wyberton by Richard Ireson

Print of the Parish Church in 1846

It is quite likely that the good news of Christianity first came to Eastern England, and even Wyberton, with Roman soldiers converted to the faith before being posted to Britain. There are no documents to chart the early beginnings of Christian worship in the village. However as you enter the Parish Church, the building takes you back many centuries and is a reminder of the generations of people who have worshipped God for over 900 years.

Bibles written in English were first used soon after the Reformation in 1530. The first record of one in the village is in 1577. Before that time the faith was taught by what people heard, could see and practice. As a result the early Church building was certainly more colourful than it is today with wall paintings and stained glass in the windows. It is very likely that there was a rood screen with a large crucifix and figures of Mary and St. John and other statues. These were used to teach the faith to people who could not read or write; feasts, festivals and pilgrimages also helped. The introduction of English bibles then changed this method of presentation. The 'King James' version was published in 1611 and used in St. Leodegar's Church until 1928. Similarly the Book of Common Prayer was revised several times before settling down after the 1662 edition.

During the period of the Civil War and the Puritan Commonwealth that followed, the non-conformist elements of Christianity prospered. Congregationalists, Quakers and Baptist groups were established in Boston but Wyberton had to wait until the nineteenth century for an alternative denomination. The Anglican, John Wesley had begun a mission in the previous century which in due time gave Wyberton the two Methodist chapels which were active until 1939.

In Victorian Wyberton the Christian faith was very strong. The church and chapels were deeply involved with the welfare and education of the villagers as well as with their souls. Most people were active Christian worshipers and it was an integral part of society.

This pattern altered forever with the First World War, increased mobility, prosperity and the secularization of society and its institutions. Today, in Wyberton as elsewhere, the Church again finds itself in a missionary situation. It continues to take an active role in fostering Christian influence and practices and its presence is greatly appreciated by the community.

St. Leodegar's Church, Wyberton by Alison Austin

Driving through Wyberton on the new A16 and you could be forgiven for turning off to the west if you were looking for the church, thinking that this would take you into the middle of the village. Instead you must turn down Causeway East and follow it for half a mile before you find yourself in the centre, both geographically and historically, of Wyberton. Climb out of your car in Church Lane and immediately you find that you step back in time into a serene, leafy village lane who's character has changed little over the last two hundred years. Still the church is elusive, retiring behind the trees, but as you walk through the gate you encounter the neat and unpretentious church building.

As you follow the path to the door at the base of the tower the graveyard is bordered by a simple flower bed, as though making its inhabitants feel at home in their garden. Two small stone angels keep guard as you approach the door. Open it and step inside.

Once you have entered the church you are faced immediately by the simplicity of the building. Your eyes are led straight to the altar, set in a small apse. There is no chancel, the nave takes you directly to the altar steps. Either side are two massive pillars, leaning outwards, thrusting up as though there should be something much weightier to support.

You have been standing under the tower. Go down two steps and look around. There are no other doors, no side chapels: it is just a single room. On the walls, a few memorial tablets, high on a window ledge are a couple of stone faces, but it is all very low-key; it is as though there is something hidden, waiting to be discovered.

This is where the present day must wait and we look back to see what has made this church building as it now is. What history is there to uncover? The clues are all around.

Wyberton had a church almost a thousand years ago. The Domesday Survey of 1086 tells us so. The church building that we see today is more recent than that, being mainly of the 13th and 15th centuries. It is unusual in that it is one of the few churches in this country dedicated to the French bishop, St. Leodegar. However we tell his story elsewhere in this book. We know nothing of the original church. It might well have been a wooden construction but the one that replaced it was much larger than today's building. We know that this church consisted of a nave and a large chancel, transepts and at least two chapels. The tower was at the centre of the church. It had what is called a cruciform shape. One morning in 1419 John Stokes, the rector found that the tower had collapsed and the nave was reduced to rubble. Only the chancel remained almost intact. The rest of the church needed to be rebuilt and a London stone mason, Roger Denys was engaged for the purpose. It was stipulated that he had to re-use the fallen masonry. The tower was rebuilt at the west end of the church. This may have been as a precaution or maybe it was a more usual layout at this period. For centuries there was a 'scratch' sundial on the *inside* of the tower as a result of this change in position! The floor level was raised by a couple of feet, possibly to try and strengthen the foundations as part of the church is built on wet clay soil but perhaps also to keep out flood water.

St. Leodegar's in 1999

All was well until 1760 when the rector Dr. John Shaw found that the pillars in the chancel were leaning at an alarming angle and feared that another collapse was imminent. He obtained permission to demolish the chancel and, because of the large size of the rest of the building, replace it with a smaller structure. At that time he was having the splendid front of the rectory built, so he took the opportunity of having the same builders do the work on the church. Hence the rather curious Georgian brick apse that is such an unusual feature of St. Leodegar's.

The next crisis occurred the following century when again there were severe problems with subsidence and several parts of the building had to be propped up to stop them collapsing. In order to properly strengthen the foundations it was necessary to undo some of the work that had been done 400 years earlier and get underneath the raised floor to do the underpinning. This is why there are two steps down into the main part of the church. At this time the layout of the earlier building was revealed and, with the floor level being lowered it leaves visible today the piers of the original pillars that would have supported the tower. These are to be seen by the lectern and the pulpit. It made an ideal opportunity for the old wooden pews to be removed. This time the restoration was carried out under the instruction of an architect called George Gilbert Scott. The work took so long that the Rector Charles Moore died, aged 93, before it was completed in 1881. Two porches and doors were removed from the sides as they were considered unsightly, leaving the church with just the entrance under the tower. Tastes in fashion change and there were clearly plans to rebuild a chancel and so the windows in the apse were blocked up as a temporary measure.

We move to the 20th century and further underpinning was required in 1916 when there was evidence of more subsidence. This is something that is regularly looked for whenever the church building has its quinquennial (5-yearly) inspection. In 1956 two stone heads were dug up in the graveyard. These were identified as being of Norman origin and are probably all that remains of the Domesday church. They are called corbels and now sit on a window ledge in the north aisle. In 1973 the interior of the church was transformed by the re-instatement of glazing in two of the apse windows. Thanks to a bequest it was possible to purchase sections of the east window of St. James' Church in Boston which was being demolished at that time. The simple figures in stained glass depict St. James and St. Guthlac on the left and St. Hugh and St. Botolph on the right. Over recent decades some of the Victorian glazing has been replaced by clear glass and now the church interior is regularly bathed in sunlight.

The jigsaw puzzle is nearly complete. We are ready to put the pieces together. Standing in the church today, the tower and the main part of the building were put up in 1419 using the stone work from the 1200's. The roof above, with its wooden angels, is the original one from 1419 but the floor beneath our feet is that of 1881. At the east end is the Georgian apse of Dr. Shaw from 1760 in which are set the windows bequeathed in 1973. Looking down from their ledge are the two guardians from the Norman Conquest. Outside the church, on the South wall, can you find the ancient scratch sundial?

As recently as August 1997 there was another potential disaster when the tower was struck by lightning. This rent some of the masonry and badly damaged the roof of the tower. The repairs have now been completed but, as with any historic building, maintenance is an on-going story. In the case of St. Leodegar's Church much of what has taken place has been well documented and so we are able to trace the evolution of this building from its medieval beginnings right up to the present day.

The interior of St. Leodegar's in 1990

The Parish Church from the East

Saint Leodegar by Richard Ireson

St. Leodegar at Lausanne Cathedral

Saint Leodegar, known as Ledger, is the patron saint of the Parish Church in Wyberton. He is also sometimes known as Leger or Leodegaruis and was born in 616 AD in present day central France. He was educated at the court of King Clotaire II by a Priest of Poitiers chosen by Dudon, Leodegar's uncle and bishop of that city. He became a deacon at twenty and archdeacon soon after. Once ordained Priest he became Abbot of Saint Maxient which he reformed by introducing the Rule of St. Benedict.

He was chosen as Bishop of Autun by Bathild, the regent of Anglo-Saxon origin. His appointment followed a long vacancy and put an end to the strife and bloodshed caused by rival candidates. He ruled as a reforming bishop; building churches, caring for the poor, holding synods, but also, like other bishops of his time, fortifying the town and becoming involved in secular and court affairs.

In 673 when the regent died Leodegar 'backed the wrong horse', became at loggerheads with the ruling house and was banished from the diocese. Restored for a short time to his episcopate his enemies eventually caught up with him and Leodegar surrendered to avoid bloodshed. He himself was blinded, mutilated and finally beheaded in 679 AD.

Although his death was for political reasons, he was regarded as a martyr. A cult centred on his tomb at Saint-Leger in the Pas-de-Calais and on Saint-Maxient, to which his relics were translated in 682, spread rapidly in France. His cult also came to England before the Norman Conquest and became well established as a feast day in the monastic calendars and in the English Sarum Rite on 2nd October. The fact that our church is dedicated to a Frenchman may be due to the fact that Count Alan of Brittany received Wyberton as part of his reward after the Battle of Hastings. The family seat was established at Richmond in Yorkshire. The last Duke of Richmond to be a Patron of Saint Leodegar's was in 1535 so there was a connection for nearly 500 years.

We can trace three other ancient English Churches dedicated to him apart from Wyberton; St. Leodegaruis Basford, Nottingham; Ashby St. Ledgers, Northamptonshire and St. Leodegar Hunston, Chichester Harbour, West Sussex. He is represented on screens at Ashton and Wolborough in Devon. But the famous horse-race is not named after him but in honour of a certain 18th century Colonel!

Rectors of Wyberton

Year	Rector
1218	Richard de Kavendis
1221	Haco
1241	Gerard de Burgh
1246	Hugh de Stow
12—	Henry de Hadelgham
1271	Henry Gomier
1281	Peter de Bisenturia
1293	Phileretus de Istro
1313	Gerard de Custancia
1320	John de Quegnon
1321	John de Lacy
1324	Hugh de Wallingsford
1344	John de Lenk
1349	John de Newbery
1360	William de Dighton
1365	Richard Claymonnd
1376	Richard de Swyneshead
1390	Henry Paristorp
——	Robert Wermyngton
1411	John Aluent
1412	Robert Rolleston
1413	John Lidyngton
1417	John Stokes
1422	John Ryder
14—	John Gigur
1502	Thomas Gibbins
1506	Gabriel Silvester S.T.P.
15—	Andrew Long
1535	Hugh Cotton L.L.B.
1540	Thomas Launcelyn
15—	Jerome Phillipps
1558	John Tailforthe
1605	Ralph Calverley B.A.
16—	William Simonds S.T.B.
1616	Robert Usher
1618	Robert Sannderson S.T.B.
1626	Richard Harvie M.A.
1667	Joshua Scargill
1671	Thomas Monleverer
16—	Moses Moore
1681	Samuel Tooley A.M.
1712	Thomas Shaw A.M.
1743	John Shaw L.L.B.
1789	John Myers
1821	Martin Sheath M.A.
1859	Charles Moore
1881	Wm. Beatson Dunning
1908	John Edmund Sedgwick
1912	Fredk. Bourne Marsland
1936	William John Ford
1942	George Boardman M.A.
1946	John Thomas Lewis
1950	Leslie Gordon Standley
1955	Derek F. Gunn
1963	Richard J. Davison
1986	Richard H. Ireson

The United Reformed Church

The United Reformed Church is situated at 232 London Road, Wyberton, on the corner of Tytton Lane East. It was officially opened and dedicated on 18th May, 1991. At national level the U.R.C. was formed in 1972 when the Congregational and Presbyterian Churches were united. At local level it is a continuation of the Red Lion Street Congregational Church.

Methodist Chapels by Alison Austin

Methodism was formed by John Wesley towards the end of the 18th century, originally within the Anglican Church but later it became a church in its own right. However it was subject to internal disagreements and division and the three main groups in this area were the Wesleyan Methodists, the Primitive Methodists and the Wesleyan Reformers (later Free Methodists). Although the Wesleyans and the Wesleyan Reformers were active in Wyberton the nearest Primitive Methodists were at Kirton End.

There are two disused Wesleyan Chapels in Wyberton that are still standing, one on West End Road and one on Streetway. Although they have both been closed for over half a century there are people who remember going regularly to them for Sunday School. Both Chapels were part of the Boston (Centenary) Methodist Circuit. Statistics concerning all places of worship were recorded on 31st March 1851 when an Ecclesiastical census was carried out.

A Wesleyan Society was formed some time before 1821 and the first chapel erected on West End Road was built in 1826. This proved too small and it was replaced by a new one in 1849. It is not known whether this was built nearby or on the same site. The building was used exclusively as a place of worship, and consisted of a single room with seating for 90 and a raised pulpit. In the census it is recorded that there were 30 Sunday School scholars and congregations of 35 and 30 respectively at services in the afternoon and evening. Zachariah Kinsley, a farmer living on West End Road, signed this return in his capacity as Class leader. In the 1930's Mr. Minns who lived next door was in charge of the Chapel. Jim Jackson and Mrs Horrey both remember going to the Sunday School and recall that Anniversary celebrations were held in a large barn in the field alongside and afterwards there would be tea and sports. The last service was held there on 22nd October 1939 and the building was sold in October 1944 for £51. 5s. Today it is in use as a joinery workshop.

The Wesleyan Society in Wyberton Roads was formed in 1822 but the Streetway Chapel was not erected until 1877. It was a small building with a single room. There was a central gangway and polished wooden benches. At the front was a raised pulpit with an organ on the right. Several former residents of Wyberton Roads recall going to Sunday School there earlier this century. (At this time Mr. Parker was in charge of the Chapel, Mrs Rushden played the organ and Mrs Hughes was the Sunday School teacher.) All spoke of the Anniversaries when they would be in their best dresses and would recite pieces they had learnt by heart. Afterwards tea would be in Mr. Parker's barn and then they would play in the grass field alongside. The last service was held in this Chapel on 28th April 1937 and it too was sold, fetching £72 in June 1944. Today it stands rather forlornly in the middle of fields and is used as a store.

Also mentioned in the Ecclesiastical Census is a school belonging to the Wesley Reformers. This was erected in 1847 and on the evening of 30th March 1851 had a congregation of 50, but the average for the previous month was supposedly 100. This was not used exclusively as a place of Worship but was also a day school attached to a house. Research has shown that this was on the Donington Road (now Ralphs Lane) and is thought to be on the site of the semi-detached houses, nos. 7 and 9. Retired Blacksmith, Jim Sharp recalls the cottage that was demolished in 1955 having an unusually large room at the back. In 1851 Alfred Jackson, then aged 12, from the Hammer and Pincers attended this school and his grandson, Jim, still has his arithmetic exercise book. The schoolmaster, Charles Millhouse, has added a footnote on the census return that *the room has been closed for a month and would be unlikely to be opened for any more preaching.* It is not known how long the school was in existence but it is interesting to note that only four years earlier the same Mr. Millhouse was paid by the Select Vestry as Sunday Schoolmaster at the Church.

There are references to other *Preaching Places* but these would be rooms in people's houses rather than separate buildings.

The old Methodist Chapel on West End Road

The old Methodist Chapel on Streetway

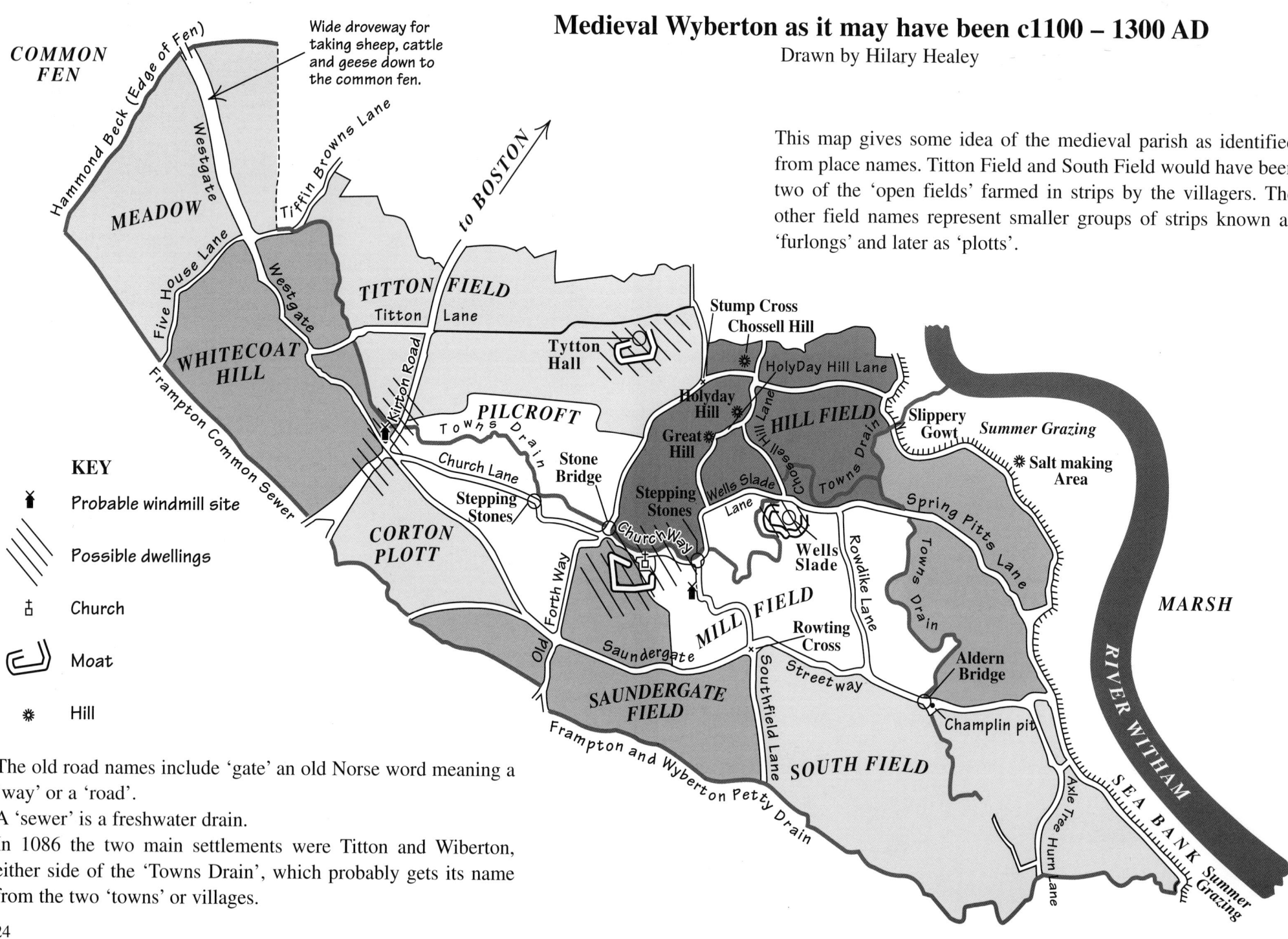

Farming

Agriculture by Richard Austin

At the close of the twentieth century the 3500 acres of the parish are farmed by about twelve farmers, most of whom have large areas of land in other parishes. Wheat is the main crop together with a small area of winter barley. There are usually about 200 acres of oil seed rape and a similar amount of vining peas. The area of potatoes grown has fallen dramatically in the last forty years to about 100 acres per year, due to the heavy nature of the majority of soil. However, on the lighter silt soil there are about 200 acres of sugar beet together with a similar area of brassica vegetables. There is just one fruit grower remaining who has apples and gooseberries. As far as livestock is concerned there is only one beef farmer and the last dairy herd was sold in the 1960's. There is one commercial pig herd and the last poultry unit has just closed.

All this would have been a great surprise to previous generations as it represents a big change. So what was their pattern of farming?

From 1860 onwards every farmer was, and still is, required to submit a return of the cropping and stocking on his farm to the government. Prior to this our evidence is drawn from about 400 probate inventories which go back to 1539. They list personal possessions in great detail at the time of death and, as virtually everyone farmed, these lists help to determine the farming pattern.

From the Tudors to 1750

By the time Henry VIII died in 1547 the citizens of Wyberton had evolved a farming system which was to remain largely unchanged for 200 years. Almost every family was a self-sufficient small farming unit. Even if they had a specialist trade such as carpentry or weaving or were merely described as a labourer, they were still part-time farmers.

During this period the parish supported about 70 to 80 family groups and it is estimated the population was fairly constant at between 350 and 450. For example an informal census in 1641 shows that there were 132 males over 18 years old in Wyberton. Typically each family kept sheep, cattle, horses, pigs, geese and hens, and had an area of cultivated land.

Many sheep were kept, usually about 40 per family rising to 100 by 1700. These figures disguise a wide variation. For example in 1541 Roger Clemond of *'Wells Slayde'* had 710 sheep and lambs in his flock.

A usual number of cattle was ten and this varied little over the 200 years. The cattle were important in several ways. Milk seems to have been used principally for cheese making and almost every household owned the necessary equipment. To a lesser extent they were also used for ploughing and hauling carts. Their meat formed an important part of the diet and their dung was dried and burnt as fuel.

Horses averaged about six per family. They were used for riding, haulage and farm work. Some were sold for the multitude of carrying and carting jobs in every village, town and city.

During this 200 year period sheep numbers in the Parish are likely to have peaked in excess of 3,000 head, cattle 800 and horses over 400.

Virtually everyone had a few pigs but rarely more than four sows were kept. Salted bacon was an important part of everyone's diet and it was a custom which persisted until about 1950.

A few hens and a cock seemed to be listed amongst every villager's possessions throughout this period. Geese are less often mentioned, however some individuals had commercial flocks. In 1611 Christopher Courtbie had about 85 geese and ganders which he is likely to have grazed in the Great Fen. They were valued mainly for the great volume of feathers and quills for pens which they produced. They were plucked live several times per year for sale to merchants in Boston where, over time, a significant feather industry developed.

There are also two early references to turkeys. In 1590 Richard Wilkinson had six turkeys. His probate inventory lists *'sex turkeis and all other pullyne vi shillings'*. Again in 1615 the Rector lists *'turkeis'* in his possessions. Can Wyberton boast to have the first records of turkeys being kept in the County? Turkeys were first introduced into Europe from South America in the early 1500's by the Spanish but it took about 100 years before they became a common Christmas dish in England.

Livestock was so important because it was the main source of food and there was usually a market for any surplus animals and their products. Before there was a railway in 1848 cattle, sheep and even geese were driven to markets as far away as Nottingham or even London. In 1696 Christopher Memet reported that droves of fat oxen and sheep were herded from this area to London *'week by week'*. Some were shod with metal shoes for the walk.

There were plenty of bees in Wyberton at this time. It was usual to have one or two hives but in 1612 it is recorded that Edmond Langrack owned *'syxe stockes and swarmes of bees'*. As sugar was a rare and expensive item honey was prized to enliven the diet.

The area under cultivation was small, however most families grew barley and to a lesser extent rye for bread. Wheat flour gradually became more popular for bread making as this period progressed and the area grown gradually increased. Beans were grown as commonly as barley and were clearly an important part of the staple diet but peas are rarely mentioned. Barley was also used for making beer. The first reference to potatoes being grown in Wyberton is in 1714 when it was recorded that Henry Dickinson had *'a parcell of pottatoes'* valued at 5s. 0d.

Hemp was widely grown in small plots by many of the villagers for its fibre. This was spun into clothes, sheets, sails and ropes. A smaller area of flax was also grown for this purpose.

The reclaimed area of Wyberton was about 2400 acres. The author estimates that probably no more than about 400 acres was cultivated for the growing of crops. The rest was permanent grass for the large numbers of livestock. The stocking rate was probably as high as was possible at the time. This in turn limited the size of the community. The controlling factor was shortage of grass in times of drought, for when there was no grass animals either died of starvation or had to be killed. Even in 1868 J.W. Robinson of Tytton Hall wrote in his memoirs that many sheep and beast had to be slaughtered prematurely because there was nothing for them to eat due to the severity of the drought. Also when the stocking rates became too high disease sometimes decimated the animals. For example, in May 1747 an outbreak of the virus disease Rinderpest, otherwise known as cattle plague, killed 6628 out of 11867 beast in the Kirton Wapentake (of which Wyberton was part). Periods of excessive rainfall also brought problems such as in the 1730's when sheep rot was common.

The common grazing on the sea marsh and inland on the Great Holland Fen was most important to farmers. Animals were identified with a parish brand. With the growth of livestock numbers the common land became very overgrazed in a dry season.

There was much unrest and disquiet when the drainage and reclamation schemes of the Great Fen threatened to reduce the area of common grazing. The first big threat occurred in 1657 with the digging of the South Forty Foot Drain with an outfall, as now, into the Haven at the Black Sluice in Skirbeck Quarter. This was an ambitious scheme to drain 36,000 acres of Holland Fen. The work met with great opposition and was largely destroyed by the 'Commoners', as the graziers were called. Thus the pastoral tradition of the parish remained largely intact and it was to be another 100 years before Wyberton's common grazing was again threatened.

Cartwrights' herd of single suckled beef cattle 1999

16th century Wyberton was not headed by a wealthy squire, as was common in other areas of the country, but rather by a group of *'middling rich yeoman'*. In 1580 a traveller in the area lamented *'the want of gentlemen here to inhabit!'*. It was then an area of small holdings with about 60% under 5 acres and very few over 20 acres. They were, almost without exception, fragmented with small plots of land scattered over the parish just as had been the case several hundred years earlier in the Saxon era.

1750 to 1870

From 1750 to 1870 was a prosperous period, with grain prices rising to new peaks. The population of the locality and the UK was expanding rapidly and new industrial towns increased demand for food. New technology and ideas were introduced and this area was in the forefront of some of these developments. Improving roads and the new railway system in 1848 proved very beneficial for the agriculture of Wyberton.

Hoeing weeds in wheat c.1900. Emma Scrupps, Mrs Ward, Mrs Fox, Lil Perkins, May Johnson, Mrs Andrews, Jack Williams.

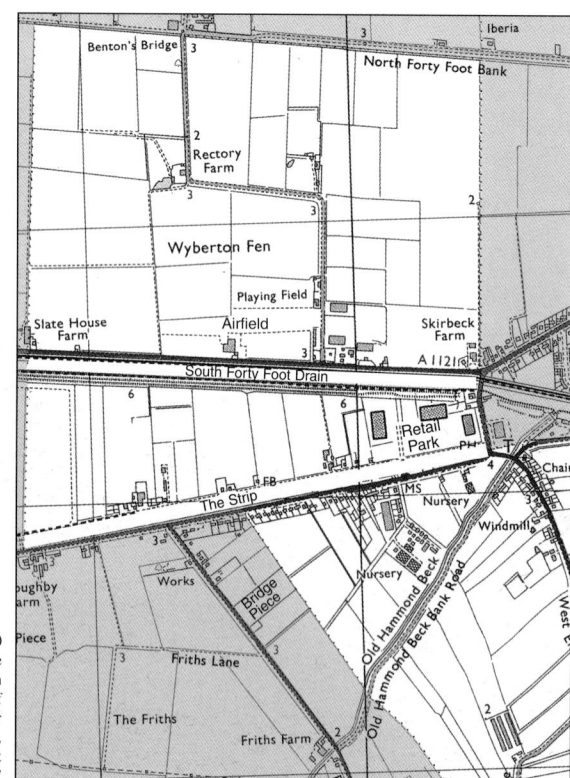

Wyberton Fen

"Reproduced from the 1980 Pathfinder 1:25000 Ordnance Survey map by permission of Ordnance Survey on behalf of the Controller of Her Majesty's Stationary Office, © Crown Copyright MC 0100014566."

A dramatic sign of better times for Wyberton was the revival of the plan to drain the Fen. This is the area to the North of the Old Hammond Beck where B&Q, Tesco, Oldrids Downtown, the Rugby Club and Airfield are now sited. An act of Parliament in 1765 allowed for the enclosure and draining of 22,000 acres of Holland Fen known as the Great Fen. Despite petitions against the proposals, including one signed by the Rector, the Rev. John Shaw, the work began. The South Forty Foot and North Forty Foot drains were the main waterways to be improved and reconstructed, and they used the same outfall into the Haven as was used in the previous century. The scheme was completed in 1800 and added 891 acres to the parish. This is the area now known as Wyberton Fen. Rights of common grazing were abolished and individual farmers purchased or rented the land which was now enclosed by dykes.

Before the drainage scheme the Commoners were not happy with the communal grazing. However they were very upset at the prospect of losing their rights as is summarised in the following letter which was published at the time. The commoner who called himself a *Native of the County* wrote: *'He lived almost entirely by the commons. He kept his cattle, sheep and geese there; he fished, he caught fowl and he gathered fuel there. These things gave him independence and he would not be compensated for their loss'.*

Potato planting c.1920

Artificial fertilizer began to be used for the first time in the form of bonemeal (ground up bones) or 'Guano' (dried bird droppings). Large quantities of the latter were imported from the Peruvian Islands in the Pacific in 12 stone (150kg) hessian bags. Even though it began to be replaced after 1900 by mineral fertilizers, all fertilizer was commonly referred to by the farming community as 'Guano' as late as the 1960's. Fertilizer was produced locally at a factory at Hubberts Bridge owned by Hammonds.

When a fen such as that at Wyberton had been reclaimed the general practice was to turn it over to arable cropping which gave a greater profit in order to pay the high rents. The first crop was invariably coleseed which is now called oilseed rape, however the first laborious job was to pare away and burn the old matted herbage and tussocks. Coleseed is a vigorous crop and will largely smother any remaining rough grass. It was both grazed and harvested for its seed which then, as now, was crushed for its oil. The residual 'cake' left after crushing was sold as cattle and horse fodder. Several crops of oats were then usually grown followed by more coleseed and then wheat.

Fortunately for the Commoners, their fears of destitution were largely avoided. There was ample employment in the drainage and reclamation work, more jobs on the larger farms and a host of activities related to the Napoleonic wars.

Field drainage made big strides forward in this period. Boundary dykes were improved and some of the first underground field drains installed. However Wyberton had a major problem with its main drainage channel, the Towns Drain. For centuries this vital drain had two outlets. One into the Hammond Beck at the north end and one into the Haven at Slippery Gowt in the centre of the parish. (The word 'Gowt' is an old English word for outfall.) The civil engineering works in The Haven in 1841 caused this drainage outlet to become silted up and useless. For a time this was a big set back to the otherwise improving situation and it was only resolved by litigation.

New crops and methods were introduced into the parish. More wheat, oats and potatoes were grown. It was during this period that crop rotations became the normal practice to the benefit of all the crops involved. An example would be: turnips - oats - beans or peas - wheat and back to turnips again.

Ridging potatoes c.1920. Arthur Willerton with Jolly and Captain

The sea marsh also yielded more arable land to the parish in this period. From 1864-1866 an area of 300 acres was enclosed. Land was also reclaimed about this time in the Haven as a result of the straightening of the river.

The first comprehensive survey of the cropping and stocking of Wyberton was made in 1866 as part of a National census. Every occupier of land was required by law to make a return in June of that year and it has been an essential chore for every farmer and grower ever since. This first survey showed the cropping to be:

Crop	Acres
Wheat	762
Barley	68
Oats	134
Beans	120
Peas	200
Potatoes	144
Turnips and Mangolds	94
Rape and Cabbage	56
Fallow	60
Clover and ley	178
Permanent grass	1053
	2869

Cropping in 1866

The improved drainage, enclosures and crop rotations enabled more livestock to be kept per acre of land and be better fed. Improved breeding techniques also helped. Some cattle were even herded by drovers all the way from Scotland to be fattened in the district.

Agriculture in the Twentieth Century

Following a period of depression at the end of the 1800's the Wyberton farming scene changed very dramatically in the 20th century. The major influences for these changes were the easier transport of produce to markets all over England and increasing mechanisation of manual tasks on the farm.

An early big change was the ploughing up of 500 acres of grassland in the first half of the century.

Reg Andrews dragging potatoes c.1935

By 1907 the area of potatoes grown had increased to 396 acres and this trend continued for the next 40 years. During the two World Wars it was because of the great demand for home grown food and between the wars it was one of the few crops that could be grown at a profit. In 1948 the area of potatoes grown peaked at 842 acres which was 40 % of the arable area of the parish. After this there was a rapid decline for two main reasons. The soil-borne pest, potato cyst nematode, was beginning to devastate yields because potatoes had been cropped too frequently and the difficulties of growing potatoes on the clay soils of Wyberton became more apparent. By 1988 the area of potatoes grown in Wyberton had fallen to 158 acres. This area has continued to decline as the complete mechanisation of the crop and higher quality specifications from supermarkets dictates that the crop is grown on easier working soils.

On the other hand the area of wheat, barley and oats has remained fairly constant at between 900 and 1100 acres for the last 100 years. Oats however were largely fed to horses which seemed to need about one acre per head. When horses were replaced by tractors in the 1950's very few oats were subsequently grown. Until recently about 25% of the cereal area was being sown with spring barley. However better wheat yields and improved autumn cultivation techniques have dictated that today mainly winter wheat is grown with some winter barley.

Legumes have been an important crop in the parish for at least 500 years but many fields have been persistently overcropped. For example in 1866 there were 200 acres of peas and 120 acres of beans growing on 1500 arable acres. This has resulted in a build up of soil-borne disease which still devastates some crops drilled now. The Bardney and Spalding sugar beet factories opened in the 1920's. The area of sugar beet grown was 28 acres in 1928 but it quickly rose to about 200 acres which is roughly the area grown today. Greens and vining peas have increased with the improved road transport, packing and cool chain facilities. 355 acres were recorded in 1943 and this area has remained fairly static to the present day.

Orchards and soft fruit have been an important part of village life since the 1880's. In the 1878 census 13 acres was recorded and by 1888 it was 35 acres. This has remained fairly constant for one hundred years and given seasonal work to four generations of village folk. For the first half of this century the main customer for the strawberries was the local canning industry. In about 1918 German prisoners of war were used to plant fruit trees in the London Road area. Today the sole fruit grower is C. DeAngelis and Son who have about 40 acres of fruit, mainly apples and gooseberries, with a lesser area of plums and pears. At one time they could claim to be one of the largest gooseberry growers in the country.

Livestock

There have been big changes in livestock this century. There were about 1000 sheep at the beginning but since then they have declined gradually until none were recorded in 1958.

Beef cattle have remained more static with 404 recorded in 1889 and 493 in 1958. Numbers, however, have fallen rapidly and now only one beef producer is left, currently with about 120 animals. Ken Cartwright and his family are continuing a very ancient Wyberton tradition. Dairying was important at the beginning of the century with 203 milking cows in 1898. It remained so until after the Second World War when the small herds in Wyberton dwindled to nil by 1970.

Until about 1960 pig numbers in the parish varied between 300-500. Since then intensive units boosted numbers from time to time. The one remaining pig farmer is Andrew Sawyer on West End Road who has about 1200 animals. Poultry are a similar story with numbers being about 10,000 in the first half of the century. Then there was a very large increase due to intensive production methods in the 1960's. In 1978 the number of birds peaked at 62,392. After that there were was a decline and the last intensive unit closed in 1998.

Potato picking c.1914

Haymaking 1933. Bob Galley with Ray and Elsie

The Mechanisation of Wyberton Farms
by Alan Dawson and Richard Austin

The mechanisation of the agriculture of the parish began in about 1840 with the invention of the threshing drum and was largely complete by 1980 by which time the use of gang labour for potato picking had become a rare sight. The transition took about 140 years from start to finish.

The most fundamental change was from horses to tractors. Horses were able to plough and cultivate light silt soils quite adequately but were often incapable of ploughing some of the clay soils of the parish. The first tractors were petrol driven and were used in Wyberton soon after the First World War. By 1919 Henry Tunnard was using a 26 horse power International Junior tractor on his Wyberton Marsh land. Soon afterwards W. Dennis and Sons also began using three wheeled French-made Scemia tractors on their Streetway farms. In the 1920's there was a big increase in the area of potatoes grown, much of it on heavier soil which had been permanent pasture. The early wheeled tractors played a vital role in the heavy work created by this change.

Threshing, Streetway c.1920. Note the 18-stone sacks of wheat

Horses, however, continued being widely used for everyday tasks on Wyberton farms until after the Second World War. In 1945 there were still 144 horses, which is nearly as many as there had been in 1869 when they were first recorded in the parish statistics. The big development came when Harry Ferguson began to market the superbly engineered small and convenient 'Grey Fergie' tractor in the 1950's complete with its hydraulic lift. This triggered a rapid change. By 1958 only 40 horses were still used and none were recorded in the 1968 census.

Steam engines also played an important role in the early stages of the revolution. Portable engines, which had to be pulled from farm to farm by horse, provided the power to drive the newly invented threshing drums. Pishey Thompson in his 'History of Boston' conjectures that the first movable steam driven threshing machine was constructed at the Phoenix Foundry in Boston in 1841. Tuxfords were also major players in the change. They sold the first combined threshing and dressing machine which dominated the market for many years. These machines quickly replaced the labour intensive and inefficient hand-held flail for the majority of corn threshing by about 1855. They considerably reduced the cost of knocking grain out of ears of wheat and other cereals. Self-propelled steam engines were a natural progression from the portables. By 1861 specially designed engines had been perfected for ploughing using a cable system; one at either end of the field to winch the plough or cultivator first in one direction and then in the other. However the use of steam engines in this way was only ever on a small proportion of the cultivated area.

Steam engines and their tackle were very expensive so were usually owned by contractors such as the Dawson family. Samuel Dawson acquired a set of steam threshing tackle in 1856. He moved from Boston to Causeway House in the 1860's. This business prospered and by 1896, when son Joseph was in charge, they acquired a ploughing and cultivating set. At the 1939 Lincolnshire Show his son, also called Joseph, purchased a 28 hp one cylinder 2-stroke Marshall M diesel tractor. This tractor was to become the contractors' favourite for driving threshing drums until the combine harvester made them obsolete. The last steam engine to be used for driving a threshing set was used on the farm of Percy Fulcher on Silt Pit Lane in about 1953. It was owned by Mr. Swain of Fishtoft.

W. Dennis and Sons were one of the few farmers in the area to own their own steam engines. They acquired their first engine in about 1910 and were using them until the 1950's. A pair of their engines was last used for ploughing in 1955.

Cutting corn was another major task which was changed in the latter part of the last century. Before 1860 all cereal crops were cut with a scythe or sickle. In the mid 1800's the first sail reapers were developed which cut the standing corn with a reciprocating knife and laid it onto a 'bed' behind. A rotating 'sail' then swept it off the bed onto the ground in a bunch ready to be tied up as a sheaf. Wilkinson Wright and Company built reaping machines at their Phoenix works in Boston and staged a demonstration at Mr. Short's farm on Streetway in 1861. Five train loads of farmers came from all over the country to this event! (This is the same Mr. Short who grew woad.) Similarly machines for hay making were developed.

The first combines were used for harvesting cereals in the Parish in the early 1950s. Contractors Dawson and Sons bought two Massey Harris 726 combine harvesters for the 1954 harvest and after a few years owned no fewer than eight of various types. In time favourable tax incentives encouraged farmers to buy their own machines. By 1965 it became uncommon to see binders, stooks, corn stacks or threshing machines in the parish. The combine had replaced them all.

The mechanisation of sugar beet lifting occurred between 1950 and 1955. The change from close drilling cluster seed to the precision drilling of single seeded pellets in the 1960's was also a revolutionary development which aided the complete elimination of hand labour in this crop.

The use of agrochemicals has probably had the greatest impact of all on the mechanisation and efficiency of the agriculture of Wyberton. The first products to be sold by the local merchants Hardy and Collins were MCPA and 2-4D for the control of poppies, thistles and other

Dodman engine at Wyberton Roads c.1880. Note the wattle farm building

Cultivating engines with flagmen, Sleaford Road c.1896. Joseph Dawson in bowler hat

Portable engine threshing, Wyberton Fen c.1910

broadleaved weeds in cereals. Noel Holgate recalls that these chemicals were first trialled tentatively in about 1950 and by 1955 were in general use by most farmers. Peter Clarke remembers first spraying MCPA in 1954 onto a wheat crop to control thistles and poppies on the Causeway farm owned by his father 'Bertie'. Herbicides for other crops rapidly followed, greatly reducing the need for tedious and laborious hand work and other cultivation. Today the sprayer is one of the most important machines on every farm in the parish. However one plot of land, farmed by A.E. Lenton Ltd of Wyberton Marsh Farm is, in 1999, being converted back to a non-spraying regime in response to the higher prices currently being offered for 'organic' produce.

The last major task to become mechanised was potato picking. The first machines made a tentative debut in about 1955 but it was 1970 before they largely replaced hand picking and the mechanical revolution of the agriculture of the parish was completed.

William Cartwright on International Junior tractor 1919. H. Tunnard's land at Wyberton Roads

Bill Meeds on Track Marshall 55 crawler at Rectory Farm 1975

The Mechanisation of the Farms of Wyberton 1840 to 1980

Period when totally or mainly used	———————
Period of transition	- - - - - - - - - - -

Horses
1953 — — — 1965

Tractors
- - - 1919 - - - 1953 ———————————

Steam Engines *for cultivating*
- - - 1864 - - - 1890 ——————— 1928 - - - 1935

Portable Steam Engines *for threshing*
- - - 1845 - - - 1855 ——————— 1890 - - - - - - 1944

Steam Engines *for threshing*
- - - 1864 - - - 1890 ——————— 1940 - - - 1953

Scythes
————————— 1870 - - - - *For limited use such as cutting field corners and headlands* - - - - 1955

Sail Reapers
- - - 1860 - - - 1870 ——————— 1890 - - - 1900

Self-Binders
- - - 1880 - - - 1900 ——————————————— 1965 - - - 1980

Flails
————— 1855 - - - - *For limited use such as beans or mustard seed* - - - - 1922

Threshing Drums
- - - 1845 - - - 1855 ——————————————— 1965 - - - 1980

Combine Harvesters
- - - 1954 - - - 1965 ———————

Potato Digging *with hand forks*
————————— 1890 - - - - - - 1914

Potato Spinners *(and Hoovers from 1930)*
- - - 1980 - - - 1890 ——————————————— 1970 - - - 1980

Potato Picking by Hand *into baskets*
————————————————— 1970 - - - 1980

Potato Harvesters
- - - 1955 - - - 1965 ———————

Sprayers
- - - 1955 ———————

1840 1850 1860 1870 1880 1890 1900 1910 1920 1930 1940 1950 1960 1970 1980 1990 2000

Hemp by Richard Austin

For at least three hundred years up until the eighteenth century most people in Wyberton grew Cannabis (Cannabis sativa). However there is no evidence that the hallucinogenic properties of this plant were realised. The common name for this plant is hemp and it was grown, together with some flax, for the fibre in its stem. This can be extracted from the stem after the soft tissue has been rotted away in water, a process known as retting. One estimate is that 15% of the arable area grew hemp in 1560 and it was commonly grown in cottage gardens. It would have been a dramatic sight in the parish as in June and July as it can grow at the rate of two inches per day and achieve a height of well over ten feet. Spinning it into fibres for making sheets, rough clothing, rope and sailcloth was a subsidiary occupation in most households. There are several references to weavers living in the parish but none to a rope maker. However there is a track known as 'Ropewalk' at the end of Wyberton Low Road near Newton's Corner. This is a place where ropes were spun.

In 1790 King George III was paying a considerable bounty or subsidy of 3d. per stone for hemp fibre. In the next century cheap imports caused a sharp decline in the area grown and by the time of the first crop census of the parish in 1866 none was recorded for Wyberton.

R. Autin in a crop of hemp

Woad by Richard Austin

Woad has been grown in South Lincolnshire since before the Tudor period as a source of blue dye. The name 'Woad Farm' or 'Woad Lane' is a typical clue to the former location of this small scale industry.

In Wyberton in about 1850 John Short began growing the crop on Streetway and built processing facilities in his yard opposite Wyberton House. Woad is a biennial crop which grows only foliage for the first year after sowing. In the second year it produces yellow flowers and then seed on stems 4-5 feet (120-150 cm) long.

The leaves have a similar shape to those of the primrose plant only much larger. They were plucked in summer by hand and taken to the mill in the yard for crushing. This was achieved by four heavy iron wheels rotating round a circular trough. There can be no doubt that the early source of power would have been horses, but it is known that a steam engine was being used when the plant was closed down in about 1903. The crushed leaves looked and smelled like cow dung. Women then were employed to form balls of it by hand, about the size of a small football, although being formed wet they

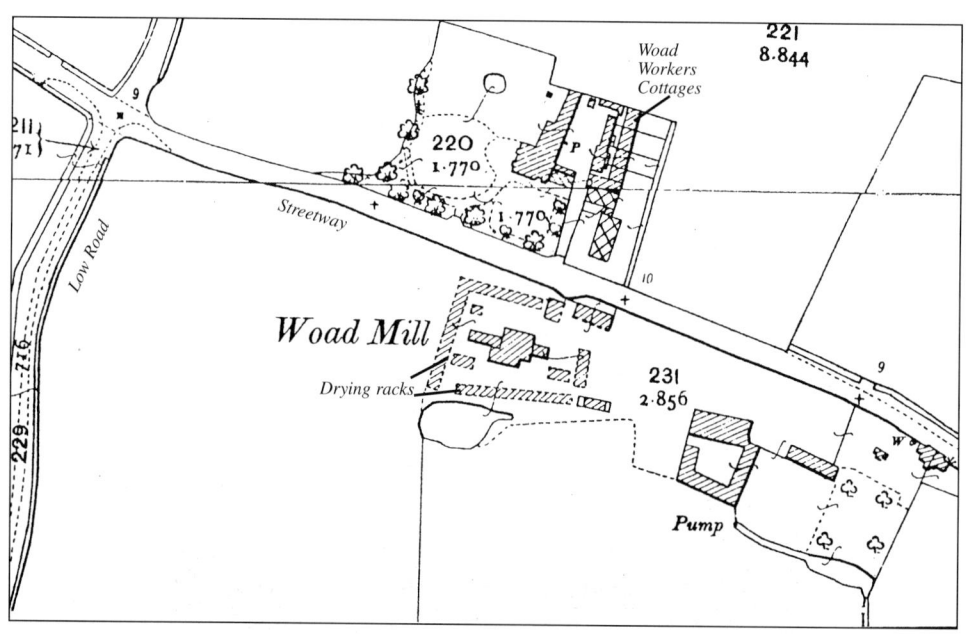

Map showing site of the woad farm in 1887

became flattened. This job caused hands to be stained indelibly black. The balls were then put on trays which in turn were placed in roofed, three-tier drying racks in the yard. These were called the Woad Range and the balls were left to dry until the end of the year.

After Christmas the dried balls were taken to the 'Couch House', broken up and spread on the floor to a depth of about three feet. Water was then added and the woad at this stage was called 'couch'. A six to eight week fermentation process then began with frequent turning and some degree of temperature control. The smell of couch was strong and unpleasant. Old inhabitants of Wyberton related that the workers largely kept themselves to themselves. No doubt the lingering smell in their clothes and houses was one explanation!

After 'couching' the fermented woad was packed tightly into barrels for dispatch by horse and cart to Boston Station. From there it was sent by rail to the cloth mills of Yorkshire and Lancashire or even for export.

Most of the woad workers lived on the opposite side of the road to the plant in a community of about eight, now demolished, cottages. In 1851 there were 15 men from these cottages working in the woad mill.

Site of Woad Mill 1999

Women outside the Woad workers cottages

Woad drying racks at Skirbeck 1921

Milk in the Twentieth Century by Richard Austin

F. Galley delivering milk 1936

In 1999 most people buy their milk from the local supermarket. Typically it is purchased once or twice a week and stored in the fridge. However for most of the century doorstep deliveries were the norm. CO-OP and Dairy Crest still make some deliveries in Wyberton, taking milk from large herds anywhere in the UK; but it is a declining business.

The story of Fred Galley's business, and his father's before him, on Causeway summarizes what has happened.

In 1928 Robert Galley took the tenancy of the small cottage at the double bend on Causeway with a few grass fields behind. His new landlord was Mr. Lister. He bought three or four milk cows from a cattle dealer, Mr. Harry Cartwright, and milked them by hand in a shed behind the cottage. With the help of his 18-year old son Fred he then built up a small dairy in the parish.

There was plenty of competition. At that time about 60 roundsmen delivered milk in the Boston area using bicycles or pony and trap, otherwise known as 'milk floats'. The roundsmen had their own organisation to fix the price of milk and control quality which was known as the Boston and District Dairymen's and Milk Sellers' Association.

On his first day Robert sold eight pints at *tuppence ha'penny* each (1p). Robert and Fred got up every morning at 4.30 am, seven days a week, without the aid of an alarm. The first job was to fetch up the cows from the field. This was not a difficult job as the animals were looking forward to high protein dairy nuts which were put in the manger of their stall in the cowshed. Each cow took about 10 minutes to milk. Fred recalls sitting on a 12 inch high stool with his head tucked well into the cow's flank so as to discourage it from kicking. After cleaning up and returning the cows to their grazing field it was time for breakfast. Doorstep deliveries began at about 7.45am, whatever the weather or day of the week. Fred usually delivered milk on his bike with two buckets of milk, one on each handlebar. Robert had a pony and trap which at first carried wide 17 gallon churns of milk to refill the delivery buckets. After the war they were replaced by the handier 10 gallon churns. A pony soon learned the milk round and it would move from one customer to the next with the minimum of command and no other guidance.

At each house milk was ladled into a waiting jug, usually covered with a muslin cloth, using either a pint or half pint measure. These hung on the inside of the bucket after use.

Afternoon milking was at about 3.30-4pm, after which some customers required a second delivery. Anyone who has experienced the delightful taste of milk straight from the cow will know why! When the Galley family moved to Causeway in 1928 there was no mains water; it all had to be drawn out of the well in the yard. It was therefore not possible to cool the milk so, in warm conditions, it would not keep for much more than 24 hours before going sour. With the coming of mains water in the 1930's a ribbed milk cooler was installed in the dairy behind the cottage, which improved the keeping qualities of the milk in the summer. In these early days there was no electricity so oil lamps were used for lighting. Mains electricity was installed in about 1930.

The increasing consumption of milk was in part due to government publicity about it's nutritional value. During the 1939-45 war, when the national diet was rather restricted, these matters were given even greater prominence and this helped to expand the Galley's business. At the beginning of the War 'school milk' was introduced, with every child being given one third of a pint (0.2 l) per day. In addition the population of Wyberton was increasing as new houses were built. In 1931/32 the Council built the row of houses in Causeway and those at Bunkers Hill, and in 1950 work commenced on the Parthian Avenue Estate.

There was always a problem matching milk production with sales. If Mr Galley was short he either bought some from another roundsman or from a creamery in Boston. There was, however, always concern about the quality of milk. It was not unknown for some producers who were short of milk on a particular day to add water to make it go round. To combat this practice Local Authorities employed inspectors to check milk at random. Fred Galley remembers having samples taken by a Mr. Fidling who lived on London Road. Occasionally an errant milkman would 'accidentally' spill his milk if Mr. Fidling appeared. Soon after the end of the War it was considered more hygenic to deliver milk in bottles. Mr. Galley recalls that the first type he used had a relatively wide neck with an internal rim which secured a card disc. Because birds soon learnt how to open these, they were superseded after a few years with bottles with a narrower neck which had a silver foil top

Milking time, Galley's corner on Causeway 1955

London Road Dairy, Ralphs Lane c.1955

clamped to the outer part of the rim. The conversion to bottles dictated changes in the delivery system, bikes with carrying frames back and front were acquired. This enabled 70 one pint bottles to be carried remembers Fred's son, Ray. In the 1950's vehicles became more readily available and the Galleys eventually bought their first van, an Austin A40. In due course this was changed for an eight horse power Morris Minor.

The Galleys built up their milk round and also the size of their herd to eight or nine cows. They needed more grassland so they hired the field opposite the Church. This had a deep old well about 15 yards behind the old cottage buildings, from which Fred had to draw copious bucketfuls of water with a rope for the cattle.

Robert Galley died in 1943. However Fred's eldest daughter Elsie stepped into the breach on leaving school at 14 and helped to continue the business. Two years later Ray also reached the age of 14 and left school.

A cow usually had one calf each year. After calving she gave a flush of milk of about 3 gallons (14 litres) or more per day. Her yield of milk then gradually declined until she was 'dried off' and rested for about a month before the next calf was due. Nine months before that she had to be served by a bull when she came on 'heat', usually known as bulling. This involved driving the animal along the road to a neighbour with a bull. This was usually the Clay Brothers who had a dairy herd and delivery round on Church Lane at 'Carlton'. After the war the Milk Marketing Board set up an AI (artificial insemination) service. Mr Ladds, the local AI man, then became a frequent visitor.

By 1960 Fred and Ray Galley were delivering to about 500 households each day. They decided to sell the cows and purely deliver bottled milk provided by Seamans Dairy. In all this time they never had a milking machine for their herd although these started to be in common use from about 1950. The Galleys finally sold their milk round to Seamans in 1975.

Others supplying milk in the parish had similar stories to tell. Charles Walter began milking cows in 1931. At first he relied on a roundsman with a bike to whom he sold his milk. However the roundsman got into his debt. To solve his problem the delivery man left his bike, cans and record book at his gate and disappeared. And so the Walter's milk round started. By the 1950's it was called the London Road Dairy and had moved into substantial premises on Ralphs Lane.

Other milk producers who had milk rounds in Wyberton during this period included: Messrs Bedford, Blithe, Garwell and Fovargue.

Mrs Wortley c.1900

J. Garwell and A. Yates sawing logs 1960

Killing the Pig by Alison Austin

In 1938 Cyril and Jenny Colam lived in a semi-detatched house in Tytton Lane East. They were not farmers but like anyone else who had the room, they kept a pig in their back garden. In fact they kept two pigs but one belonged to their neighbour, Mrs Lennon, who worked at Calders. "Pig" potatoes were cooked by boiling them in an old copper and were mixed with the meal and any kitchen waste in a galvanized bucket. This was then fed to the pigs in their sty. During the years of rationing a portion of a family's meat ration would be given up in order to buy pig meal.

The first pig was killed in November and the second about six weeks later. Both families shared the two animals. This way it made the supply of meat last much longer. Most villages had a butcher or special pigman who went round killing the pigs and cutting them up. Mr. Cowan, the landlord of "The Pincushion" would come to do the Colam's pig. Daughter, Joyce Colam, recalls how the killing, by cutting the throat, always conveniently happened during the daytime when she was at school and that she would return home to find the pig stretched out on a special board called a cratch, where it was washed with boiling water and its bristles scraped off. After this it was hung up in the garden on a large tripod called gib poles, being hoisted aloft with a block and tackle. When it was cut open the blood was collected in a bowl and the carcase was disembowelled, the intestines being used for sausage skins. The blood from the bleeding throat was made into black pudding. As the meat was cut up some was jointed and the best hams were covered in butter muslin and hung on the kitchen wall. The rest of the bacon was salted and hung in the pantry. Then all available hands would be set to work in the kitchen where brawn and sausage, pork pie and haselet were made. Pork was minced with herbs and breadcrumbs and forced into the washed intestine which would be twisted into links of sausages. These too would hang in the pantry as this was before most households had a fridge.

Joyce's job as a young girl was to take round a plate of "pig cheer" to each of the neighbours. This would consist maybe of "fry", some liver, kidney and heart, perhaps some skirt or even some sausage. It was tradition that the recipient of the cheer removed it onto another plate and returned the other one unwashed. You would receive similar plates of cheer as other neighbours killed their pigs.

In a family where there were boys the prize was the pig's bladder. When washed and dried this would be blown up and kicked around as a football.

All Lincolnshire folk know that no part of a pig is wasted. The only bit of the animal not used is its squeal!

Jenny Colam at 40 Tytton Lane East c.1950

Wyberton School, Low Road c.1948

The Community

Parish Affairs   by Alison Austin

In the 18th and 19th centuries each parish was responsible for administering many of the services that are now provided by the local authority. This task fell on the shoulders of a group of around twenty suitably qualified parishioners known as the Select Vestry who would meet once a year to elect the Parish Officers for the ensuing twelve months. These would then meet regularly in the Church to carry out the many duties required of them. The most important of the officers were the two Churchwardens, who were responsible for affairs of the Church and the maintenance of the building. The Vestry Clerk was the individual who kept records of all meetings and elections and received a salary for this work. He would make up the Account books for the other officers who included several Overseers of the Poor, two Assessors of Taxes, the Surveyor of the Highways, two Dikereeves and anywhere between two and six Parish Constables. One notable Vestry Clerk for Wyberton was Juba Page who held the office for thirty years until his death in 1843 and who also was a Parish Constable from 1815 -1842. In the Churchyard there is a gravestone for him erected by the Rector at that time, the Rev. Martin Sheath. The Vestry Clerk would affix all notices to the Church door. This was the parish noticeboard. Until 1862, when the National School was built, the Church was the only public building. It served as the office for virtually all parish affairs and as the parish meeting place.

Overseers of the Poor

The most onerous of the parish duties was that of the Overseers of the Poor. These parishioners included two assessors of taxes whose task was to collect the rates agreed annually by the Vestry from all occupiers of land within the parish and calculated according to the rental value of their holding. For the year 1813 -1814 this assessment was eighteen pence in the pound but it generally varied between 2s. 6d. and 4s. Every month a dozen or more of the poor would come to the Church where the monthly *Collection* would be made. They would receive an appropriate amount of money depending upon whether they had a family to support or were a widow. Typical payments were:

July 7th 1816: Dixson 16s.
  Hornby 8s.
  Phillips 14s.
  Horns Family £2.
  Rose & Child £1. 6s.
  Anderson's Child 10s.

Additional payments were made in between distributions as necessary. Also the vestry would regularly order that household items were supplied or repaired.

Jan 29th 1800 *Kettle for the Poor House*
June 23rd 1816 *Thos. Holbourn: a Tin Boiler*
Dec 21st 1817 *Waltham: 1Blanket, 1Rug for the Children's Crib*
  Saul Tibbs: Pair of Sheets
Dec 13th 1819 *For Robert Rose Shoes mending 2s. 6d.*
Nov 21st 1835 *Borrell: a Wash Tub 3s. 6d.*

Clothing was distributed to the poor twice a year although items were frequently supplied at other times, especially shoes and children's clothes. May 22nd 1829 is referred to in the Vestry records as *Cloathing Day*. Where there was someone in the family capable of dressmaking, appropriate materials would be given for the required garments. In other cases the material was given to another poor person in the village who was then paid for making up the clothes. This is just one of the situations where the poor were employed for the benefit of other members of the community and paid out of the money collected by the Poor Rate.

Clothes worn by a woman included a gown or frock, a shift, a pair of stockings, a flannel petticoat and an apron and a pair of shoes. Then there are frequent references to *Tydies* (thought to be knickers), a pair of stays and a bonnet. Men's clothing consisted of a jacket and trousers or breeches, a shirt and often a *slop* (a smock or loose fitting garment) and a hat. There was nearly always a (neck) handkerchief, a waistcoat, a pair of stockings and shoes or some other kind of footwear mentioned.

Bill for making clothes for the poor c.1820. Paid by the parish.

Nov 22nd 1795   Hids: a pair of Pattons (clogs) 1s. 3d.
May 25th 1800   Dixon: Cloth for 2 Shifts, 2 Aprons, 1 Handkerchief
Gray: 2 Shifts, Flannel for a petticoat, 1 Apron
Butters: 16oz of Worsted for Stockings, 1 pair of Breeches,
Oct 19th 1800   Thos. Sanderson: a pair of Highlows
May 11th 1817   Sarah Tunnard: 3 yds of Brown Cotton, 3 yds of Calico,
1½yd for 2 Tydies
Waltham: 6yd of Calico, 5yds for Tiddies
May 13th 1819   Thos. Blyth: Waistcoat, Breeches, Hat,
2 Pairs of Stockings, Slop, Pair of Hightop Shoes

Quantities of coal were purchased every year by the Vestry and distributed to the poor. In some parishes coal is known to have been stored inside the church. *Nov 14th 1823 Mrs Vinters: 1¼ chaldron of coals* (1 chaldron = 36 bushels = 1.309 cu. metres)

Occasionally a poor person would be instructed to go round and collect for some particular item. *On March 23rd 1824 it was ordered for Mrs Vinters to go out with a Brief to collect towards buying a cow and the Parish would make up what she had not been able to collect.*

Money was given regularly to families of men serving with the Militia. The Overseers of the Poor were also responsible for housing the poor and the Widows of the parish and for repairing their houses and helped pay rent in times of hardship.
Nov 19th 1792:   Thatching John Gibson's House 15s 11¼d
Apr 16th 1811:   It was ordered that Saul Tibbs' house be pulled down and rebuilt

There were occasions when a family would be moved into a house and the existing occupant moved in with someone else. The Parish owned several Poor Houses and administered Widow Houses through the various charities.

April 13th 1827: Ordered for Mrs Grummitt to be removed to Mrs Hopkin's house and Mrs Hopkin to be removed to Ann Phillips
Jan 18th 1828: Ordered for William Shringfield to be put to Mrs Hopkin and to be found a bed and to maintain himself with his pension. Also for a warrant to be taken out against Jesse Green to show why he do not maintain his wife.

Parish Workhouse

At a Vestry Held Thursday the fourth Day of July 1811 and Duly called for that Purpose it was ordered by the under signed Persons that a Workhouse Shall be Built on the Strip of Poor Land now in Tenure of Charles Darnell in this Parish.

This new Parish Workhouse is often subsequently referred to as the Poorhouses and was probably a row of five or six cottages. What is certain is that they were built for a sum of £386 3s 7½d in 1812 and that a rate of two shillings and sixpence in the pound was required to pay for it. Originally the buildings would have been thatched but by 1820 it was tiled and a quantity of bricks were used for its repair. In 1822 five new chimney pots were bought for 15 shillings. We have reference to the land lying in the Bridge Piece, which is the triangle of enclosed land between the Old Hammond Beck and the Turnpike Road to Swineshead and we now know that it was on the site of a row of cottages bordering the Swineshead Ramper that were demolished in the 1930's.

The first occupants of the Workhouse are recorded on Feb 26th 1812 and were Francis Showler and his wife and also Thomas Showler and his wife. On March 31st 1812 *it was ordered in Vestry for Saul Tibbs, his wife and one child to have harbor in the Workhouse until farther orders.*

By 1868 these six tenements and gardens were rented out and on July 21st 1874 it was decided to apply to the Poor Law Board to sell them.

The gravestone of Juba Page

Schooling

The children of the Poor were given schooling in the parish, paid for by the Overseers of the Poor.

April 7th 1799: Paid for the schooling of Tibbs Children 16s. 6d.
Nov 23rd 1818: Ordered that the poor children were put to school at the expense of the Parish.
May 6th 1822: Mrs Allam was paid for teaching 8 poor children at 3d. per week.

Sunday School was an important part of a child's life. In April of each year a sermon was preached in aid of the Sunday School and a collection then taken at the church door. On April 20th 1845 the Rev P. Alpe preached the sermon and the collection raised £8.1s.2d. out of which Mr. Millhouse was paid a half year's salary of £2.10s. Other items relating to the Sunday School that year were:

Oct 11th: Bought 3 forms, 1 table and 1 chair 10s. 6d.
             Door for the Schoolroom 3s. 6d.

Sickness and Health

If a labourer was unable to work through illness or accident he would receive temporary benefit from the Parish. The Accounts of the Overseers of the Poor record:

Oct 22nd 1799: Gibson when ill 2s. 6d.
Jan 4th 1800: Paid Thos. Day, a woadman, when ill 5s.

When any of the poor needed the services of a Doctor, this was paid by the Parish as was the cost of any medication that was required. This was not limited just to medicine or pills but included wine, brandy and opium! (Malaria was endemic in the fens until about this time and opium was used to relieve the symptoms.)

Extract from Doctor's bill for attending the poor 1760

Jan 17th 1793: Paid for bleeding the poor 2s.
July 28th 1821: Paid Dr Mason for setting Mrs Atkinson's arm 5s.
Jan 18th 1828: Paid for leeches for Mrs Overton 7s.
June 3rd 1831: Paid for opium for S. Rose for 2 weeks 1s. 4d.
Nov 26th 1831: A bottle of wine for S. Rose 2s. 4d.

In 1821 a journey to Boston was made to consult with the Doctor concerning the inoculation of the children (presumably against smallpox). In May 1827 the Vestry agreed to employ Dr Snaith as the Parish Doctor.

If possible the Poor were paid to nurse each other and to do chores for the elderly and it was regularly arranged for a woman to have assistance at the time of childbirth or *accouchement*.

May 12th 1816: H. Tompson's washing let out for £1. 1s. per year.
Jan 3rd 1829: A. Phillips for nursing E. Nicoll 14s.

Similarly they were paid for laying out the dead. Coffins and funeral expenses, which usually included the cost of a grave and a bell, were regularly paid by the Parish funds. Many of these funerals were for young children.

Aug 24th 1815: Funeral expenses for a drowned man 18s. 5½d.
June 6th 1834: Coffin for Sims 6s.
Dec 5th 1834: Laying out Mrs Watkinson 5s.
               Bearers for H. Horn 4s.
               Bell and Grave for H. Horn 6s. 4d.

Entries in the Parish records also include:

Oct 30th 1833: Buried Sarah Cook who hung herself, aged 19 years
Feb 1st 1835: Buried James Ridlington aged 41 years killed by a carthorse in this Parish.

Not all sickness could be dealt with locally. The County Hospital was opened in Lincoln in 1769. In March 1826 Ann Trafford was taken by a horse and cart to the Sluice in Boston and then to the Hospital in Lincoln by *Packett* (boat), travelling in a sedan. She stayed for a week and the total bill, including the travel and her board and lodgings, came to £3. 4s. 10d. (She died in 1829 so her treatment must have been reasonably successful!) In 1867, the then Rector of Wyberton, Rev C. Moore was appointed a Governor of this Hospital and the Vestry agreed to make an annual subscription of two guineas.

In 1820 a lunatic asylum was also opened at Lincoln. There are several records of the Overseers of the Poor having to deal with *Lunatik Papers* and writing to the Governors of the Asylum. In 1822 Ann Coward was committed to the Asylum.

Warrants and Orders of Court

A considerable amount of time was taken up with journeys to Magistrates Courts. A Parish could apply to have a Removal Order made against any poor person or family that was not able to support itself and was not entitled to settle in that parish. There are records of removals being made both to and from the parish of Wyberton. In 1793 Andrew Black was sent back to Scotland at a cost of £3. 4s. 6d. Some people managed to return to the Parish. Ann Atkinson was twice removed from Wyberton to Sutterton, once in 1833 and again in 1835! In this same year Samuel Hutchinson together with his wife and family was removed from Carrington to Wyberton.

Another official duty was that of obtaining maintenance of illegitimate children from their father. An *order of Filiation and Maintenance* required the alleged father of any bastard child to pay an appropriate sum of money every week while ever that child was in the parish. Any man refusing to pay would risk being committed to the local *House of Correction*, which was near the Black Sluice outfall on the site of Newton House in Skirbeck Quarter.

All the services mentioned so far were carried out by ordinary village men who had to fit their official duties in with their day to day lives. An army of Civil Servants and Social Workers are paid to do all these tasks nowadays!

Work

Most families in Wyberton lived a meagre existence close to the bread line. The Parish had its own version of Child Benefit:
Dec 21st 1821: at a Vestry it is unanimously agreed that the labourers in the Parish with 2 or 3 children when in work, are to subsist on their wages except where the family exceeds 3 children, in which case there will be an additional 3d per day added by the Parish.

Any able-bodied man without work who was receiving payment from the Parish could expect to be employed in some manner to the benefit of the com-

Poster for the Lincoln to Boston Packet

community. The above resolution continues: *If the labourers are out of imploy they are to be employed upon any public works in the Parish and the Officers that employ them are to pay each man one shilling per day and their wages are to be made up by the Overseers of the Poor.*

Traditionally such people were put to work repairing the roads, but in this Parish there was another important need for labour, namely the maintenance of the Sea Bank and the dykes.

June 27th 1812: Saul Tibbs mowing thistles at the sea bank 15s.
July 10th 1812: Thos. Goodacre 5 days at the sea bank 17s. 6d
Oct 24th 1812: Paid Saul Tibbs 3 days cleaning Tunnells ends 7s. 6d
June 23rd 1826: Poor men are to be employed in carting silt .... and to be allowed 18d per day.
Dec 23rd 1833: Wm. Hammond, Overseer of the Poor, is to employ such paupers as come to him for labour on the highway.
Jan 10th 1834: Men out of work to be put to work on the sewers.
June 6th 1834: The men out of employ to be set to work at the Silt Pit

One of the habitually poor members of the Parish was Thos. Blythe. In 1817 in order to pay off some of his debts he was ordered to sell his waggon and the following year he was put to J. Page until May Day 1819, to be clothed and his washing paid for. At the same time his family was also taken in: *Lucy Blythe to stop on at Mr. Dickenson's and 2s. per week be allowed with her and also Mary Blythe to stop with Mr. Minta at 6d per week.*

Bill for mowing thistles and nettles on behalf of Saul Tibbs to the Surveyor of Highways 1812

Frequently the eldest children of the poor were put into service in the Parish and a small weekly allowance made and also clothing provided. Wyberton was a parish where there were very few people who could be considered wealthy beside the Rector and the owner of Tytton Hall but the Censuses of 1841 and 1851 indicate that a large number of households had one or more servants living in. Some of these were presumably the poor who had been placed with them by the Overseers.

Apr 28th 1816: Horn's eldest girl and Holborn's eldest boy to be put in service, 1 s. per week to be allowed with each.
May 26th 1826: Agreed in Vestry for Thos. Benton to have as servant Sarah Tunnard and to be allowed one shilling per week, the Parish to find necessary clothes for one year.

Servants were regularly hired for a year commencing on May Day. Parish records for 1833 state: *Mrs Wyan agrees to take Mary Burrell as servant for one year and have necessary clothes, to take her place on Monday 29th April 1833. Also agreed for Mrs Oatley to take Ann Hall for a year at one shilling per week from this Parish and necessary clothes from May Day 1833 to May Day 1834. Also agreed for Mr. and Mrs Stanley of Skirbeck to take Ann Watkinson for a year at one shilling per week and ten shillings for clothes from the Parish from May Day 1833 to 1834.*

Apprentices

Boys were often put to learn a trade by being apprenticed to a suitable craftsman. In 1804 Sall Tibbs, who we assume is our friend Saul Tibbs, was ordered to be put out as an apprentice shoemaker until he was aged twenty one with Robert Burton. He was to be allowed twelve pounds and provided with two suits of clothes. It is not clear if Saul benefitted from this experience judging by his ensuing existence! Not all apprentices came from Wyberton itself. In 1832 the Magistrates sent Boston child, Henry Smith to be apprenticed to the Wyberton wheelwright, John Watson.

Parish Constables

Parish Constables were appointed each Easter in the Vestry. Besides having to deal with matters of local law and order they were required to deliver Warrants and similar papers and to attend the Magistrates Court. They were also charged with collecting the associated tax. An entry from the Constables Book reads:

March 20th 1753: agreed this day in Vestry that the Constable William Harwood for the year 1752 shall collect an assessment of three pence (per acre?) *for here upon all occupants of land in this Parish to defray the necessary expenses of their office...*

The number of Constables varied. In 1842 they appointed six and in 1847 it had risen to eight. In May 1892 the Vestry needed to get 6 staffs and 2 sets of handcuffs. By the time the year 1900 was reached, the magistrates only required two Parish Constables and it was necessary to collect in 3 pairs of handcuffs and staffs. The post was still in existence in 1927 when William Sharp, the Blacksmith, of Spalding Road was one of those appointed.

Another of the Constables' duties was rounding up vagrants. Wyberton had its fair share of tramps and itinerants and there are several mentioned in the Parish records.
Aug 2nd 1817:   Relieved a man with a pass for America 5s.
June 19th 1819: Paid to a tramp 2s. 6d
Aug 25th 1819:   Paid for a journey for an Irishman
Jan 17th 1820:   3 tramps on the way to Norwich paid 3s.

There were village stocks, presumably for punishment of some offenders, but we have no knowledge of their situation. Our only record comes from the Vestry account book:
Feb 2nd 1827:   A lock with 2 keys for the Stocks 2s.

Dikereeves

Not all parishes would have Dikereeves but Wyberton always had two. Their duty was to collect the Dikereeve Rate which was then used to maintain the all-important Sea Bank and the Sewers, which are what we know as ditches and drains and which were essential for keeping this low lying parish from being regularly flooded. For the year 1812-1813 the two dikereeves were James Munk and Benjamin Lamb. There were always two rates to be collected. The first was for the expenses of the Sea Bank and for that year was 3s. 4d per acre. The second, at 4d per acre, was for the expense of the sewers. The total amount collected in Wyberton with these two taxes that year was £285. 8s. 5d. For the year 1814-1815 the two rates were 16s. and 2s. 6d respectively, but this seems to have been exceptionally high and later in the century both rates were just a few pence per acre.

We have already seen that local labour was used for mowing the bank, cleaning out the ditches. Saul Tibbs was one of the regular labourers; he was kept busy in 1814!
Oct 1st :   paid Saul Tibbs for 9 days work £1. 2s. 6d
Oct 8th: paid Saul Tibbs for 6 days work 15s.
Oct 15th: paid Saul Tibbs for 6 days work 15s.
Saul was unable to write his own name as one of the receipts is clearly signed on his behalf and then contains *"X his mark"*.

The Dikereeves had to attend the Court of Sewers regularly and pay the appropriate court fees. They also regularly spent a day *riding the Sea Bank or riding the Sewers.* For all of these duties they were able to claim expenses. There are also frequent references to *taking the clow up* and, a few days later, to *putting the clow down.* The *clow* or *clough* was the sluice gate. Overseeing the repair of the bank and the sluice gate were the responsibility of the Dikereeves.
Apr 30th 1817:
for sowing seeds on the bank
2s. 6d
Nov 23rd 1818:
paid Marshall for making and hanging the clow door 16s.
Dec 24th 1818:
paid Donnel for paint and tar for the clow door 1s. 6½d
Nov 21st 1820:
paid S. Walton & Co for heightening the Sea Bank
£11. 17s. 6d
Jan 11th 1839:
paid a fisherman for picking up a wheelbarrow 6d
It is also remarkable how frequently wheelbarrows needed to be repaired!

The Dikereeves accounts also give details of all the materials

The Village Stocks by Margaret Cowe

used for strengthening the banks. In 1822, between the months of May and August, 693 tons of chalk were delivered to the Dikereeves at the sea bank by boat from South Ferriby and Gravesend, payment being made to the Captain. This was typical of the ten year period from 1816-1826 when large quantities of chalk and cliff stone were used for repairing the sea bank prior to the straightening of the Wyberton Roads section of the river. In March 1847 there are the first references to using *kidsticks* for repair work. (Kidsticks are bundles of sticks, eg brushwood, that help to stabilize the slope of a dyke or bank.)

Highways

The Surveyors of the Highway were the Parish officials who collected the tax levied on Lady Day each year for the expense of keeping the public roads of the Parish in good repair. For the year 1758-1759 the highway tax for Wyberton was 3d per acre. The Surveyors also had the duty of employing such labour as was required for the repairs and of obtaining the necessary materials as well as overseeing the work.

From Tudor times the Government had made each parish responsible for its own roads. Parishioners were supposed to work gratuitously for six days each year on the roads and farmers were to supply two men and a cart. This was known as *boon work*. However by the middle of the eighteenth century it had become customary for many people to make a payment in lieu of carrying out this labour. The parish then passed on appropriate moneys or *composition* to the Commissioners of the Turnpike.

In 1759 it was recorded that a Causeway was to be laid down from the Church to the milestone on the Turnpike road. Previously this road had been referred to as *Church Lane* but this is clearly the origin of the present name, *Causeway*. There had been problems with this section of road which was very low lying and muddy as there are frequent references to placing stepping stones along it.

The Rector is twice recorded as helping out financially. In 1838 and 1839 the Rev M. Sheath lent money for parish roads to be shingled. As well as repairing the roads in 1863 the Surveyor of Highways was ordered to fence the Parish Well which was on the north side of West End Road, alongside the public highway. With the coming of the Railway there were more complaints. This time, in 1883, the highways were thought to be dangerous because of the steep incline where they crossed the GNR rails.

The Highway fund sometimes appears to have been put to other uses however.
Mar 31st 1876: money allowed out of the Highway fund for the maintenance of an additional teacher.

Soon after this date highways ceased to be the responsibility of the individual parishes.

Parish Council

On June 22nd 1894 a meeting was held to make preliminary arrangements respecting the Parish Councils Act. It was agreed to form one Ward and to have one Polling Station. This was, in due course, to be at the National School Room which was at that time in the centre of the Village. Today the centre of population is around the Pincushion and polling takes place in the Parish Hall.

The Minute Book of the Parish Council opens with the following words: *The first Parish Meeting held on Tuesday the Fourth day of December 1894 in the National Schoolroom Wyberton for the purpose of selecting Seven Qualified Persons to represent them on the Parish Council, there was about Seventy*

Lloyds Garage, London Road 1949

*Electors present. Proposed by James Brown and Seconded by the Rev W. B..Dunning that John Short take the Chair, carried Unanimous.....*and so Wyberton's first Parish Council came into existence.

The seven councillors elected were:
Arthur Samuel Black, Farmer, of Skirbeck
James Brown, Gardener, of Wyberton
James Burrill, Farmer, of Wyberton
William Lane Claypon, Gentleman, of Tytton Hall
Samuel Dawson, Machine Owner, of Wyberton
George Henry King, Labourer, Nr Wyberton Church
George Ward Wright, Fruit Grower, of Skirbeck Quarter
(At this time Skirbeck Quarter was part of Wyberton Parish.)

At the first Council meeting, held on 31st December 1894, Mr. A. S. Black was elected chairman and J. Dawson was appointed the Parish Clerk. A few months later, in April 1895, Mr. Arthur Cooke Yarborough, Solicitor of the Cottage, (now 211 London Road) Wyberton was elected the Chairman, a position that he was to hold for thirty eight years until his death in May 1933.

Parish Business in the 20th Century

After 1894 Vestry meetings were mainly concerned with church affairs and in due time this body became the Parochial Church Council.

Initially the Parish Council affairs were dominated with appointing the Dikereeves and fixing the Dikereeve rate and dealing with matters relating to allotments and Charities. Parish boundaries were fiercely guarded but there was some amendment as a result of the straightening of the Haven at the end of the last century and in 1909 Skirbeck became quite separate from Wyberton. A regular feature was the arranging of appropriate celebrations whenever there was a Coronation or Jubilee. The Council's imagination appeared only to stretch as far as *Tea and Sports* on every occasion!

Business took on the now familiar pattern of discussion about street lighting, building Council Houses, the state of the sewers, road repairs etc. 1932 saw the building of the first Parish Hall on London Road, which was in turn replaced by the modern one in 1985.

In the War years Parish meetings were held in Mr. Avery's house on London Road which had become the First Aid Post. A Parish Invasion Committee was formed in 1941 and a specially fitted out Decontamination Hut was erected by the Military at the rear of the Parish Hall. *The Parish Hall was to be kept for casualties as the First Aid Post was only fit for cases who did not require a stretcher. Iron Rations were stored at Lloyds Garage* (on London Road). The committee decided to hold an Invasion Exercise: *Mrs Goffin asked for some more bandages. It was agreed to have plenty of casualties...*

Mrs Andrews at the Almshouses on Church Lane c.1950

A momentous victory for the village was the opening of the new school on Saundergate Lane in 1957, the old school having been totally inadequate and unfit for many years. (The population of Wyberton had leapt dramatically from 829 in 1931 to 1809 in 1951.)

At the census in 1991 Wyberton is recorded as having a population of 3906. It has 1552 households and 1607 dwellings and the Parish covers an area of 3237 acres. This last figure has not changed much but the Parish has come along way since the year 1801 when its population was a mere 477. Two hundred years ago Wyberton was a small, self-sufficient rural community where many of the population lived a precarious existence on the brink of poverty. The centre of village life was the Church, from which all the Parish services emanated. Today, as we step into the new millennium, Wyberton is a prosperous cosmopolitan place, fighting to stay as a village rather than be swallowed up as a suburb of Boston. The self-sufficiency has disappeared, however as services are now supplied either by the Borough, the County Council or by central Government. It is to be hoped that Wyberton's residents will retain their sense of community.

Parish Councillors walking the parish footpaths 1965. J. Winter, Mrs P. Blackie, D. Frost, C. Wain, G. Woodcock, R. Brown.

Education in Wyberton by Richard Ireson

Wyberton School on Saundergate Lane currently has a roll of 240 pupils and a staff of 10 led by headmaster Mr. Bill Smith. There are 9 classrooms and extensive grounds. Education has made great progress from tentative beginnings about four hundred years ago. Education in the parish of Wyberton was first nurtured by the Church and has been sustained and developed by that influence to the present day.

Nothing specific is known of the period before 1500. However it can be assumed that the Rector was one of the few able to read and write having been trained in basic Latin and Greek for liturgical purposes. There is evidence that in association with the church or individual educated parishioners others learned the basic rudiments of reading and writing initially using the Bible and the Book of Common Prayer. Books were scarce and expensive commodities in the early years of printing. The first layman in the parish known to have owned his own Bible was Bryan Curtes in 1577. It is carefully described as an *English Bible.* However it was not until about 1630, just before the Civil War, that ownership became commonplace.

Provision for the education of children is first recorded in 1595 when William Jackson dictated : *Myne Executor (his wife) shall have the tuission , governance and keepinge of all my said children.* In 1607 William Ullyat left £14. 19s. 8d. for various things including *the educacon of the said children.*

Following this date references to *tuission* become more common, but the first mention of reading is in 1659 when Gaberell Craforth speaking of his daughter Elizabeth said: *Rafe Edwards of Becker (Bicker) shall take and keepering my daughter and bring her upp till shee accomplishes the age of eighteene yeares with learninge both in reading and sewing which is fiting for one of her ranke.*

We have the first specific reference to a charity school in Wyberton in the early 1700's based on a subscription system paid by supporters. The school was directly influenced by the Society for the Promotion of Christian Knowledge formed in London in 1699. This institution provided education on a large scale for both sexes. It is likely that the Revd. Samuel Tooley MA and the father and son Rectors Thomas Shaw and John Shaw LL.B., an educated and cultivated succession of incumbents of Wyberton at this time, would have been involved in this development. The location of the school room is a matter of speculation. Perhaps it was in the Church or in the extensively rebuilt Rectory?

Wyberton School, 1908-9 with Miss Rumsby and Miss Robinson. Fred North back row, 3rd from right

The education of the poor children was the responsibility of the parish. In the early 19th century we have frequent references to women in the parish being paid for the tuition of children. Possibly they were widows or dames teaching a few children in their own homes. A typical weekly amount seems to have been about 3d. per child.

One form of education that the Church provided was Sunday School. It was financed every year by a special service held at Easter, a collection being taken at the church door. It often befell the Curate to preach the sermon on that occasion. Records show that Charles Millhouse was being employed as schoolmaster at a salary of £5 per annum in 1845 and 1846. In 1846 a new door for the schoolroom cost 3s. 6d.

Arithmetic book 1851 belonging to Alfred Jackson

Miss Patchett's (Mrs Lowther) class c.1920

It was interesting to note from the 1851 Ecclesiastical Census that the Wesley Reformers had a school at Wyberton erected in 1847 and attached to the home of Charles Millhouse on Donington Road, Wyberton (now Ralphs Lane). This implies that he changed his employer to teach at this new school but it was a short lived venture as there is no mention of it in the 1861 census. In 1851 twelve year old Alfred Jackson from the Hammer and Pincers was attending this school.

The Revd. Charles Moore was Rector from 1859-1881. During this period he persuaded the National Society to contribute £18 towards the building of what is now known as the "Old School" on Wyberton Low Road. This was the Wyberton Church of England School and it was founded by a Deed dated 26th September 1862.

The Log Books of the "Old School" are complete from 19th June 1872 until the closure on 28th July 1961 and present many delightful insights into life in a country parish during the late 19th and early 20th centuries and to the conduct of education in the school. Mrs. Moore, the Rector's wife, regularly came into the school to hear pupils read; her daughter would teach needlework and singing. The curates and rectors came to teach geography, arithmetic and scripture. The Diocesan Inspectors for North Holland visited in order to conduct scripture, singing and recitation tests. The Rectors regularly confirmed the Head teacher reports in the log book and added their comments.

Absences due to bad weather conditions remind us of the distances some pupils walked to and from school. Epidemics of scarlet fever, chicken pox, mumps, measles and such are recorded. Involvement in work on the land is a commonly mentioned reason for absence. For example:

27th November, *1874: The family have been in the woad fields all the summer and for some weeks the two boys have been employed amongst the potatoes.*
27th June, 1919: *Closed the school today for 2 weeks – early potato picking holiday.*

Wyberton School 1999. Headmaster W.J.H. Smith with Nathan Booth and Chloe Bell, the oldest and youngest pupils

Wyberton New County Primary School opened on 11th September 1957 with Headmaster Mr. J. Scott. The two schools ran parallel for four years. In the New County Primary School log book for 27th July 1961 is recorded: *Head attended the presentation of farewell gift to Miss F. A. Tooley Headmistress of Wyberton C. P. School who retires on 28th July 1961 after 42 years as head.* A long incumbency, making her a power in the land.

After closing as a school the building was used for a Youth Group and Sunday School until 1990 when it was sold and a portion of the proceeds made into a Trust known as the "Wyberton Sunday School Fund" administered by the Rector and Churchwardens. It is indeed a delight to see how Mr. and Mrs. Fred Alexander, who purchased the Old School from Lincoln Diocese, have lovingly and carefully restored this building which has such a special place in the life of our community.

Wyberton School 1999

Sugar Rents by Richard Austin

A curious custom which persisted for over two hundred years in Wyberton was the payment of rent in both money and sugar. This was demanded by Boston Corporation for land and property which they owned or administered on behalf of various charities. The first record of the Corporation demanding part payment in sugar appears in the minutes of a meeting held in 1597. An early example relating to Wyberton concerned the lease of a cottage with 6 acres of land and 34 acres of pasture to Thomas Welbye in 1640 for ten years at £52. 3s. plus 4 lbs of sugar per year.

This became known as a 'Sugar Rent'. Was this a hedge against inflation for long term contracts in uncertain times? Is it the origin of the term 'a sweetener' as a euphemism for a bribe?

Sugar was certainly a valuable commodity in the 17th century. Sugar from sugar beet was not produced commercially in Europe until 1811 and in the UK until the 1920's. Thus cane sugar from the West Indies must have been largely used. By 1730 the usual demand was for best hard sugar. Did this indicate some poorer quality sugar of lower value was available? For example, Michael Robinson in 1737 was asked to pay *£16 plus 2 lbs of best hard sugar and the usual covenants* for a ten year lease on 16 acres of pasture.

Sugar Rents were actually paid in sugar from 1597 to 1721 and it was demanded by Boston Corporation in respect of most of their long term leases. They first became payable in cash in 1721 when the price of sugar was fixed by the Corporation at one shilling per pound.

In 1843 Sugar Rents from Charity Lands run by Boston came to about £18 and this was divided equally between the National and Public Schools. Wyberton School, built in 1862 on the Low Road, was a National School so hopefully it would have benefited from this arrangement. The custom ceased later in the 19th century. Occasionally the practice is symbolically revived by the Borough from time to time to keep an old tradition alive.

The demand for sugar in lieu of rent appears to be a custom peculiar to Boston. Extensive enquiries have failed to identify any other Borough in England which has had a similar practice.

Paying the Sugar Rent by Glynn Williams

Wyberton Mills by Hilary Healey.

Wyberton has boasted several windmills and many horse-mills in its history.

The base of the documented windmill still survives at the north end of West End Road. It was a brick tower mill, which was built about in 1800. A few early references have been found. It is not shown on the earliest map of Wyberton, dated 1791, and it seems to have had a relatively short life. In the Parish Assessment Book for 1856 Farndon Groom is recorded as both owner and occupier of the mill, John Fotheringham having been the previous proprietor. Kelly's Directories for 1900 and 1913 name Arthur Samuel Bontoft as miller (wind and steam) as well as baker, and parish records in 1907 name W. Fretwell as owner. The mill was taken down between 1915 and 1919 when the property was re-valued. Perhaps its demise was a direct or indirect consequence of World War 1.

The new brick mill would have been built after 1791, but probably quite soon after. Situated towards the end of West End Road near the newly enclosed fen it would have been well placed to process corn coming straight off the freshly cultivated land in Great, Middle and Little Fen, to the west. The relatively early demise of this tower mill is a mystery. The photograph shows it in all its glory in about 1900.

From this date it became progressively more derelict, as shown by contemporary photographs. In all of these only the brick base is shown, with one window and a makeshift roof. In 1951 it was described as 'covered with zinc and turf, and used as a chicken house'. Peter Dolman in his book on *Lincolnshire Windmills* published in 1978 states that it was built in the early 19th century and worked until the 1910s.

Allegedly the mill was once worked by John Pocklington of Heckington. It is also said that four sails from here went to Heckington.

Windmill West End Road c.1900. Note the portable steam engine aligned with pulley wheel

Wyberton Mill by Karl Wood 1951

*Postmill in Franks Lane
by Cyril Smith*

The watercolour was painted in colour by Karl Wood on 24 March 1951. Wood, a Gainsborough artist, nursed an ambitious plan to paint every windmill in the country, from which he has been nicknamed 'Windmill Wood'. He did not succeed in this, but he did complete over 200 in Lincolnshire, mostly painted in the 1930s and the 1950s. This collection is at the Museum of Lincolnshire Life.

There was a much earlier windmill which would have been a post-mill, probably on the site of the medieval mill – every village had one. It lay south-east of the church about half way along a track that leads from Church Way to Rowting Cross which is now called Franks Lane. The mound was marked on the early Ordnance Survey maps as a 'beacon', but when archaeologist C. W. Phillips visited in the 1930s he thought it might possibly be a mill mound. He was not then aware that the field south of the mound used to be called Mill Field. It is known that Edmonde Langrack owned a windmill in 1642 which was valued at £30. Was this where his mill was sited? Interestingly, there is the tradition of a mill, as well as the evidence of old millstones, along Streetway somewhat south-east of where the post-mill site lies. This is the location of a former blacksmith's workshop. There is no documentation on this mill, and it is just possible that stones came here from another site, such as the post-mill site, although movement of old millstones was not done much before this century.

The 16th and 17th century documents give us interesting snippets on horse-mills. The grinding stone was turned by a horse walking round in a circle pulling on a pole. This in turn was fastened to the top stone. There are eight horse-mills recorded in probate inventories over a 100 year period from 1560 to 1660.

*Horsemill
by
Glynn
Williams*

57

Blacksmith's Shops and Forges by Jim Sharp

The village blacksmith was once the only source of tools and equipment used by farmers and local craftsmen. The last two hundred years have seen the role of the village blacksmith evolve to reflect the development of engineering and technology. Changes, begun by the Industrial Revolution, have continued throughout the twentieth century to the present day. The large scale manufacture of tools and equipment started the slow decline in the number of village blacksmiths. Many adapted to provide a service for the repair of mass produced machinery and often-made modifications and adaptations to improve the efficiency and use of equipment. Blacksmiths and farmers together continued to develop their ideas into prototypes of new farm machinery, which were often copied by industry to supply the mass market.

Whereas in Wyberton and surrounding villages, there had formerly been two, three or four working shops at the end of the 19th century the numbers dwindled to one, and in many cases to none at all. In Wyberton the smithy at the Hammer and Pincers, where the blacksmith was also the landlord, closed in the early 20th century after being in the Jackson family for over half a century. The farm smithy in Streetway closed, probably during the First War, when the farm changed hands. There are also vague memories of a further small shop, now long gone, on Whileys Lane. The remaining busy blacksmith on London Road was situated close to the once also busy wheelwrights shop, the one complementing the other. At the beginning of this century they had a combined workforce of six to eight craftsmen and apprentices often working together in the building and repair of carts and wagons etc. and carrying out the shoeing of cart wheels. Both still employed two smiths and two carpenters up until the mid seventies. At times during the 19th century both shops had been under one ownership.

Many of the blacksmith's crafts, skills and working methods were based on methods used and passed down over hundreds of years when the smith was the main skilled member of the community. He was relied upon to provide the many goods, equipment and services required not only for agriculture and transport, but also for the home, with many still providing these well into the 20th century.

Until the end of the nineteenth and early twentieth century the horse was practically the farmer's only source of power for cultivation and transport, and it was around this that most of the blacksmith's work originally revolved. Most of the tools and cultivation equipment were therefore relatively simple, designed, made and maintained by the smith. There was also the constant shoeing of horses, a craft passed down from Roman times and still using similar methods and tools. Not only did the smith-cum-farrier shoe the horses, but, with his intimate knowledge of the horse's hoof and foot, frequently was called to treat a lame foot with a bruise or a prick. The trouble spot was pared out with a knife and a bran poultice applied over three to four days to reduce the infection. This usually required three or four visits and a leather protective pad was fitted before the horse was allowed back onto the land.

As larger manufacturers began to produce labour-saving machinery, such as reapers and potato diggers and manufactured copies of many of the tools and equipment formally made by the Blacksmith, the gradual change in farming methods also began to affect the smith. It was during this early period of change in 1916 that William Sharp took over the smithy on London Road from William Atkin who had run the shop for about ten years. The business remained in the Sharp family for almost seventy years, a period which saw

The Old Wheelwrights Shop on the left is still standing with the original Blacksmiths Shop backing on to Ralphs Lane demolished in 1936. A staff of four wheelwrights and four blacksmiths included, 2nd from left, Blacksmith Mr. Franklin; 4th, Wheelwright Mr. C. Horrey, and 7th, Wheelwright Horace Smith with daughter c.1915.

the greatest changes to the methods and equipment used by farmers and blacksmith over the past 2000 years.

The corn binder was introduced during the 1920s and was followed by the gradual introduction of the tractor. Although at first treated with scepticism by many, it was the contractor and bigger farmers who mainly realised its potential for deeper and faster ploughing and cultivation. Following orders for increasingly heavier and larger equipment for cultivation, it was in the early thirties that William Sharp installed his own power unit with a second hand four cylinder car engine. This provided power to drive a grinder, drilling machine and his own self-built power hacksaw enabling him to handle the new work and heavier materials required, particularly as the new 'crawler' tractor came into use on the farms. The smaller farm was now looking to tractors as a source of power until by 1938 there was scarcely a farmer without a tractor.

In the mid-thirties, the council decided to improve the road junction where Ralphs Lane meets the London Road. The blind corner resulting from the Smiths shop with its back to Ralphs lane had long been a hazard for the increasing amount of traffic. So it was in 1936 that the old Smithy which had stood there for centuries and with its 16 yards of back wall, used as a poster board by the "Boston Bill Posting Company", was finally demolished. Its replacement by the present building caused quite an upheaval for the smiths who were refitting equipment and tools whilst maintaining an uninterrupted service for their customers.

The Boston Gas Company was persuaded to extend its supply to this area of London Road resulting in gas lighting in the workshop instead of paraffin lamps and candles. A gas engine was fitted to power drive shafts, which in turn powered drilling machines, grinders, lathes and hacksaws.

As the tractor began to take over as the main source of power on the farm, so the number of horses for shoeing began to decline. As farming methods changed so the methods used by the smith and the type of work changed. Larger implements were required including harrows, duckfoots and rolls. Implements originally designed for horse power were adapted for use with the tractor. Three-point linkages were fitted and horse shafts removed and replaced with a draw bar. Instead of building carts the joiners were now building new lorry bodies creating more ironwork for the smithy.

Piped mains water arrived in the area in 1936-37. The blacksmith, who had for many years supplied and repaired the many lead water pumps and pipes in general use, was now licensed as plumber for laying water pipes and fitting to most of the farms and many private dwellings in the area.

At the beginning of the 1939 war the Rural Industries Bureau arranged for rural smiths to be supplied with oxy-acetylene cutting and welding equipment on interest-free credit and with free tuition. This new equipment was to bring the most fundamental change yet to many of the age-old methods and skills, speeding up and simplifying many jobs. Before this, all of the smiths forging and welding of iron and steel was done by heating in the hearth fire which was blown to a white heat by the bellows, then welded together and shaped and forged on the anvil as required. Now with the oxy-acetylene welding equipment, pieces of steel could be welded together to the required pattern without the forging. Four-inch cart tyres could be cut and welded to fit the wheels by one man, an operation previously needing four pairs of hands. Many jobs,

The Old Smithy on London Road shortly before being demolished. Harry Madison, George Priestly, William Sharp c.1935

previously impossible for the smith, could now be successfully accomplished and this became particularly important during the war years when replacement spare parts were scarce and difficult to obtain. The oxy-acetylene bronze welding of malleable and cast iron was often a vital necessity, particularly for broken and worn parts of binders and other machinery.

Although there were a good number of working horses coming into the forge for shoeing until well after the war, gone were the days when six, eight or more horses were queuing outside of the smithy waiting their turn for shoeing. This was particularly the case on wet days. With the changing work style, the smith introduced a shoeing by appointment system.

With many of the old horse-drawn carts still in use, the wooden wheels still required re-shoeing. In the old days this involved the heating of a stack of five or six cart tyres, with probably a number of smaller tyres in the middle. It required five or six pairs of hands for several hours, to manipulate the hot tyres onto the wheels, lying on the six foot circular shoeing platform. They were then quickly cooled with gallons of water to shrink the tyres, causing them to tighten to the wooden wheel. With the increasing popularity of the rubber tyred tractor, so the demand for rubber tyred trailers to be built brought a new industry for the wheelwrights and the smiths.

Although electricity has been available in parts of Wyberton and Kirton since 1926, it was after the war in 1947 before it was made available to the vicinity near the smithy. Once connected the electricity brought a new dimension to many operations. Light and power at the press of a button to work machinery, electric fan forge blowers instead of endless pumping of the bellows by hand (one set of bellows went to the Skegness Farm Museum and is still in working order). Next came the electric arc welder, more versatile, quicker and stronger than the gas welder although this still remained an essential piece of equipment. With its speed and capability for welding much heavier materials the welder reduced some of the reliance on the forge and some of the more traditional methods. The forge, however, still played a large part in the smith's working day. The introduction of the power hammer, manufactured by the smiths themselves in 1948, proved a big success, making short work of much of the heavy hammer work.

Blacksmith Jim Sharp working at the leg vice in the smithy just prior to his retirement in 1985. The anvil can be seen in the foreground with two forges, a power hacksaw and power hammer.

The Old Smithy with the first two buildings already demolished with John Clay helping out c.1936

After the death of William Sharp in 1965, Jim Sharp who after working with his father for neatly thirty years, bought the premises and continued the business and hardware retailing.

From the 1930s and into the second half of the 20th century the blacksmith had evolved into an agricultural engineer, providing a repair service for the numerous breakdowns and replacement of wearing parts to the bigger and increasingly complex farming implements. This gradual, but ever increasing tide of change transformed both farm and smithy. By the last quarter of the century teaching all but the most basic skills on the forge had become irrelevant and replaced with simpler modern methods. During the twenty years up to 1985, a number of would-be apprentices had started work at the smithy, but only two stayed to become qualified smiths. Both later left the profession to take up different trades.

Records from early in the century give the wages for an apprentice signing up for a four-year term at five shillings a week for the first year, rising to ten shillings in the fourth year. Shoeing a horse with four shoes in 1912 cost the farmer just two shillings and four pence, (now less than 12p). At the end of the century the cost is now thirty-eight pounds.

In 1985 on the retirement of Jim Sharp, blacksmith Mr Ernie Lawson who had worked at the smithy over the previous year took over the business. He was a traditional blacksmith using the modern techniques and skills of an agricultural engineer.

The century ends with the computer beginning to dominate all aspects of commerce and industry. While the present smithy has not yet taken the next step into the microprocessor based world of operation and control, it will surely come if it remains long into the next century.

At the approach of the millennium, the wheelwright's shop, which had also served as the village undertaker for many years, had already been closed for ten years, after being in the family of H. Smith for over eighty years. The future of the last Wyberton Blacksmith's Shop, when the present smith, Mr. E. Lawson retires, and with no apprentice in sight, is not clear. This may be the end of the Blacksmith's craft in Wyberton as carried out on this site over the centuries. We must wait to see what the next century brings.

Blacksmith Jim Sharp, standing on the old wheel shoeing platform explains the craft of shoeing cart wheels to his grandson c.1985

The old wheelwright shop c.1995 that closed in 1990. Gone is the old smithy and the busy scenes of eighty years ago

Brickmaking by Hilary Healey

There must be many Wyberton gardeners who are familiar with its clay soil, although happily it does not occur all over the parish! In 1489 Boston's Corpus Christi Guild owned a field in Wyberton called Pottertoft, and it may be that a potter dug and worked local clay, but unfortunately we do not know where this was.

Bricks and tiles were being made in Boston and in some parishes by the early 1300's but we know nothing about Wyberton this early. At first brick was a prestigious building material used only by the gentry, as seen at Hussey Tower in Boston, Wyberton Rectory and nearby Frampton Hall. In 1702 there was a field called Bricks where brickmaking may have taken place, but it was in the Slippery Gowt area so perhaps they were used for making the Sluice walls since they were usually fired as near the relevant premises as possible. The bricks for the Rectory, for instance, may have been made from clay dug out of the 'moats'. In the late 18th century, encouraged both by the prosperity and the increasing demands brought on by Enclosure, brick building became widespread. By the mid 19th century there were brick makers in most Lincolnshire parishes, and Wyberton is no exception. Three sites have been identified here. Information comes mainly from the early Census records and the various County Directories.

In 1856 Charles Whitworth had a brickyard and pottery in Tytton Lane. This was sold to John Cooper of Spalding Road before 1881 and was still in his ownership in 1907. We do not know exactly when brickmaking ceased on this site. Langleys, the builders were obtaining bricks from here until the mid 1930's, but they may well have been manufactured elsewhere. In the same vicinity, but slightly to the north, was Joseph Robinson who had a brickworks between about 1892-1907. A third business was in the Great Fen, where Edward Armes (sometimes called Armes Rawden) had a brickyard. This was in operation from at least 1872 to the 1930's.

At all of these sites there were clay pits and brickyards but, because of the method of manufacture, there were not the tall chimneys that we have come to associate with large modern brickworks near Peterborough.

However in about 1960 the wife of the owner of the Tytton Lane pits, a Mrs Gostelow, spoke of there having been a tall chimney which her husband had demolished, using the bricks to build their bungalow.

Even into the present century bricks were being made by hand, the clay being pressed into wooden moulds. After slow drying in open-sided sheds they would then be fired in a kiln to the required temperature of 950-1150°C. Traditionally bricks were fired in a 'clamp', a large stack of bricks carefully placed to allow space for the heat to circulate. The clamp was covered with turf, earth or old bricks and tile and then fires lit around it. The so-called 'scotch' kiln evolved from the mid 17th century along with increased use of coal for fuel, and was widely used in 19th and early 20th century Lincolnshire. This type of kiln is a solid brick structure, but still open-topped. Doors for loading access are used at each end and a row of fireholes along each side produced even heat. Firing took 3 to 5 days and kilns operated from April to October as a rule.

When brick makers built, or had built, their own houses they often took advantage of different coloured bricks to produce decorative effects, especially around doors and windows. This was evident on the former dwelling house at the Fen brickworks on Boardsides, and in the wall at 211 London Road. Both used bricks decoratively in different ways. The Armes/Rawden bricks were reputedly very hard bricks. The last house to be built using these bricks was the bungalow at 19 Swineshead Road, Wyberton.

On the first Ordnance Survey maps the clay pits are shown as irregular shaped ponds. Those down the Boardsides have been filled in this century, but in Tytton Lane West and behind houses on London Road some still exist. These are now filled with water and have provided an amenity for fishermen.

Decorative brickwork, 211 London Road

Brick pits, Tytton Lane West

Samphire and sea lavender on Wyberton Marsh

River and Marsh

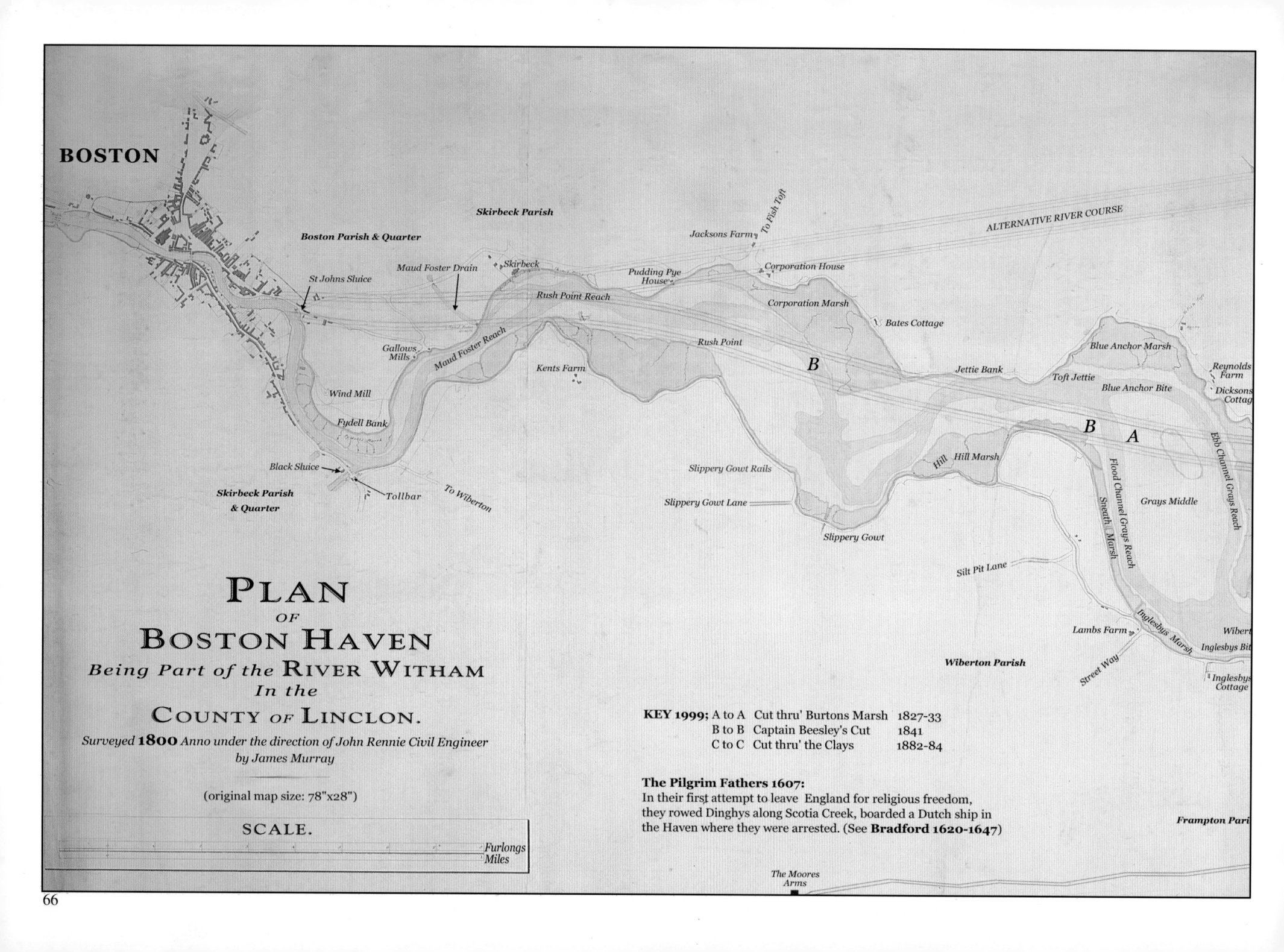

PLAN
OF
BOSTON HAVEN
Being Part of the RIVER WITHAM
In the
COUNTY OF LINCLON.

Surveyed 1800 Anno under the direction of John Rennie Civil Engineer by James Murray

(original map size: 78"x28")

SCALE.

Furlongs
Miles

KEY 1999;
- A to A Cut thru' Burtons Marsh 1827-33
- B to B Captain Beesley's Cut 1841
- C to C Cut thru' the Clays 1882-84

The Pilgrim Fathers 1607:
In their first attempt to leave England for religious freedom, they rowed Dinghys along Scotia Creek, boarded a Dutch ship in the Haven where they were arrested. (See **Bradford 1620-1647**)

Map labels:

BOSTON; Boston Parish & Quarter; Skirbeck Parish; Jacksons Farm; To Fish Toft; ALTERNATIVE RIVER COURSE; St Johns Sluice; Maud Foster Drain; Skirbeck; Pudding Pye House; Corporation House; Rush Point Reach; Corporation Marsh; Gallows Mills; Maud Foster Reach; Kents Farm; Rush Point; Bates Cottage; Blue Anchor Marsh; Reynolds Farm; Wind Mill; B; Jettie Bank; Toft Jettie; Blue Anchor Bite; Dicksons Cottage; Fydell Bank; B A; Ebb Channel Grays Reach; Black Sluice; Flood Channel Grays Reach; Skirbeck Parish & Quarter; Tollbar; To Wiberton; Slippery Gowt Rails; Hill; Hill Marsh; Sheath Marsh; Grays Middle; Slippery Gowt Lane; Slippery Gowt; Silt Pit Lane; Inglesbys Marsh; Lambs Farm; Wiberton Parish; Wiberton; Inglesbys Bite; Street Way; Inglesbys Cottage; The Moores Arms; Frampton Parish

66

67

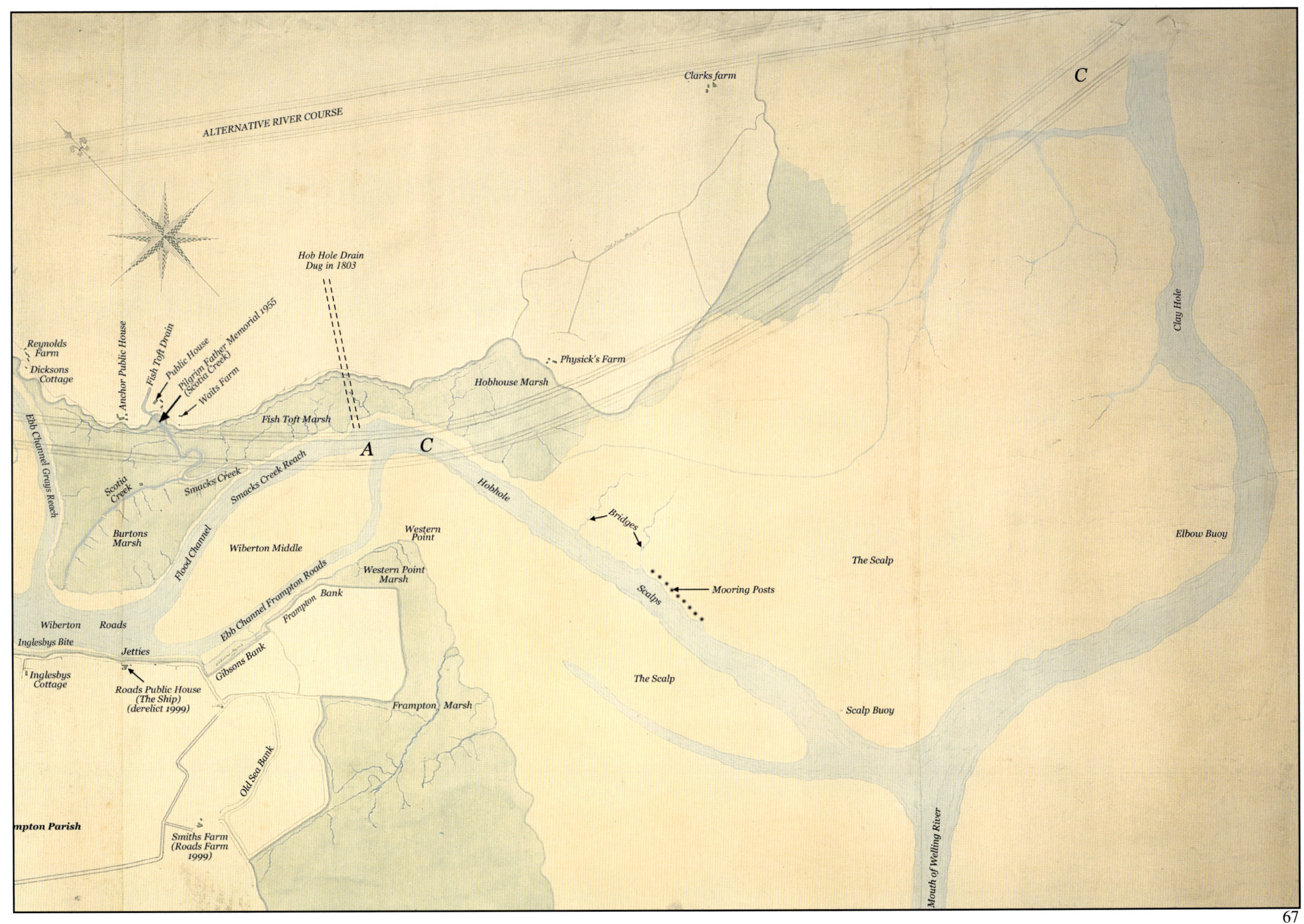

The Straightening of the Haven by Frank and Sally Bowser

In the last century Wyberton witnessed possibly the greatest engineering project ever undertaken in Lincolnshire. Today the result of this work continues to have, directly or indirectly, a beneficial effect not only on a large proportion of the parish but also on Boston and the area 15 miles to the west and north.

The Old River

The Haven is the stretch of river downstream of the Grand Sluice and it has a catchment area of 1200 square miles. In 1800 it was, as its name implies, a place of safety or refuge for shipping. However the accumulation of sand and silt was increasingly preventing the efficient drainage of about 300 square miles of land and Boston was becoming almost unusable as a commercial port for shipping. At that time John Rennie, the celebrated engineer who designed London Bridge, was commissioned to survey The Haven and draw up plans to improve the situation. The project was to create the deepest and straightest possible channel for the thirteen and a half miles from the Black Sluice to The Wash. He was also asked to ensure that silt did not collect in the section of the river through Boston up to the Grand Sluice, thus impeding the drainage of the Witham.

Most of his proposals were eventually adopted but it was to be 1884 before the last part of the work was finished. Time has proved it to be a most successful scheme ensuring that, even today, the drainage of a huge area of land is much better and cheaper than it otherwise would have been. It shortened the channel by some four and a half miles and it has also ensured the future of the Port of Boston.

Rennie's map (pages 66-67) shows a wide estuary containing a river following a very tortuous channel which was bedevilled by shifting sands. His bold pencil lines reveal his strategic plan to restrict the water course into a deep, self-scouring channel and to shorten the length of the river by some four and a half miles. For most of its length the centre of the river marks the parish boundary.

Using the modern map below it is still possible to walk the thirteen and a half miles along the Old River Bank from opposite the entrance to the Dock in Boston, right out to the Welland. The parish boundary is crossed at the Landfill Site at Slippery Gowt. After a further 1.6 miles, alongside the lane called Wyberton Roads is a derelict house which used to be the Ship Inn. This public house overlooked an extensive anchorage with jetties. Here the river was about 150 yards wide and was called 'The Wiberton Roads'. *Roads* in this context means a safe stretch of water where ships lie at anchor. The Ship Inn is at the

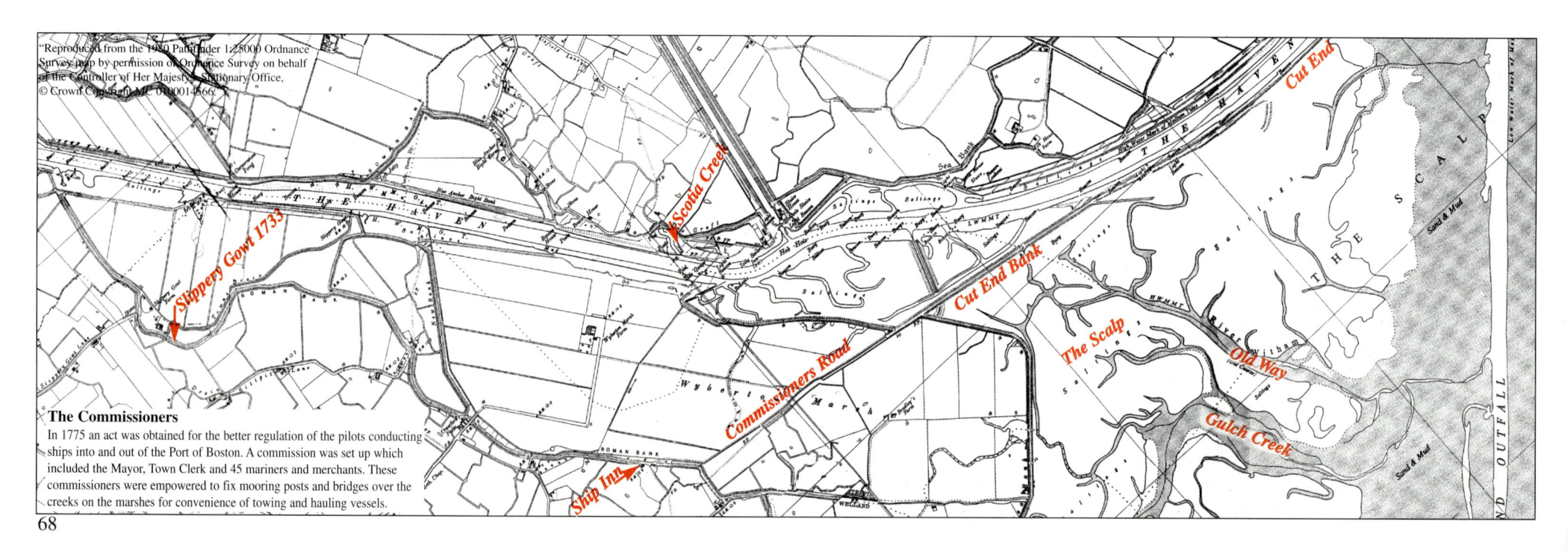

The Commissioners

In 1775 an act was obtained for the better regulation of the pilots conducting ships into and out of the Port of Boston. A commission was set up which included the Mayor, Town Clerk and 45 mariners and merchants. These commissioners were empowered to fix mooring posts and bridges over the creeks on the marshes for convenience of towing and hauling vessels.

junction of the lane and The Commissioners Road. The latter is a track which follows the line of the old river side and leads in the direction of the Hobhole pumping station.

It will be seen from the map that beyond the Hobhole the course of the old river passes beneath the present Cut End Bank some 450 yards from its intersection with Wyberton Sea Bank. Here barges and ships were sunk to help close the old channel. To follow the line of the original waterway it is necessary to cross the sea marsh known as the Scalp. This walk to the wilderness of shifting sands at the old Witham/Welland outfall should only be undertaken with an experienced guide.

Caution: Be very careful when walking on the Marsh. Refer to the tide tables printed in the local papers and liaise with the RSPB Warden.

Here, standing on the bank of the Old Way near to where the marsh grass gives way to mud and sand, it is easy to imagine the waterway at this point has altered little since the 12th and 13th centuries when ships of 300 tons sailed on this river. Then, at times, more trade passed here to Boston and Lincoln than up the Thames to London.

From the proud heights of the 13th and 14th centuries Boston suffered a decline and our story starts in 1751. In that year an engineer named Nathaniel Kinderley alluded to the desperation of the Port when he wrote a report saying: *'Boston Haven is worse than it was ever known to be; for whereas thirty years ago, a ship of two hundred and fifty tons could get up to Boston town, now, even a small sloop of forty or fifty tons, and which draws but six feet of water cannot sail to or from the town but at spring tide'.*

The Straightening of the Haven

The fascinating story of the straightening of the river that now follows is best told by refering to contemporary engineers' reports.

In 1800 John Rennie was directed by the Corporation to report his opinion on the best mode of improving Boston Haven. He attributed the condition of the river partly to the Grand Sluice which had been erected some 30 years earlier above Boston, remarking, *'If the Grand Sluice were entirely taken away, and the tide suffered to flow up the river, it is evident it must move with a greater velocity through the Harbour of Boston to fill the space above; it is equally evident the constant action of this great body of water passing through the harbour, would grind the channel deeper'.* He found that the width of the channel at low water varied from 82 ft near the church to 306 ft opposite Maud Foster; 429 ft at Wyberton Roads and 330 ft at Hobhole, increasing in places to 1,500 ft at high water; that the channel above Hobhole meandered through extensive shifting sands and became even worse below West Marsh Point. The water coming from the Witham and the Welland shifted its course so frequently that the channel one day was in a different place to that which it occupied on the previous day. Rennie suggested two plans for improving the river. The one by making a straight cut from Skirbeck Church to Clayhole; and the other by straightening and contracting the present channel between Skirbeck Church and Hobhole, and making a new cut nearly in the direction laid down in 1793 by the engineer Capt. Huddart.

In an 1827 Act, the Corporation were empowered to borrow a sum of £20,000 to carry out the works recommended by their engineer, Mr. Rennie. These consisted of straightening the river by means of a new cut, 800 yards in length,

The Old Way in 1999, probably as it was in 1751

Aerial view of the river at high tide below Hobhole

through Burton's Marsh, thus cutting off the great bend at Wyberton Roads and shortening the distance to deep water by one mile and a half. (Marked 'AA' on Rennie's map) The work was undertaken by Messrs. Joliffe and Banks and completed in the year 1833, at a total cost of £27,262.

The remainder of Sir John Rennie's plan, embracing the straightening of the river from Skirbeck Church to join this new cut, was not commenced till the year 1841, when Capt. Beasley undertook to train the channel, which was continually shifting between these two points, by fascine work, and to excavate, where necessary, so as to make the river as nearly straight as possible. This work he successfully accomplished at a cost of £11,627. Fascine work involves placing bundles of sticks, known as kids or faggots in the bank of the river to strengthen or build up that area by actively encouraging the accumulation of silt amongst the kids. The technique was used here on the outside of the river bends, firstly to narrow the channel and by degrees to straighten it. It was an effective and cheap method. It was cheaper than making a new cut which is probably the main reason why this line for the river was chosen as compared with the alternative route shown on Rennie's map.

Another considerable piece of training by fascine work was the diversion of the waters from their circular course round Blue Anchor Bight Marsh to a straight line carried out in about 1860 by Mr. Robert Reynolds, Surveyor to the Trust. (Marked 'CC' on the map)

These three major projects successfully straightened many tortuous bends and deepened the channel along these sections of the Haven. However they did not solve the severe problem at the outfall of the Haven where the channel passed through the Scalp. Earlier Rennie described the Scalp as *a solid and compact bank* composed of sand, gravel and clay, averaging from 10 ft to 13 ft above Hobhole Sill. Owing to this high bank, the tide from Boston Deeps could not get into the Witham Channel until about two-thirds of the flood had made, and then its force became comparatively deficient. The Drainage Commissioners had long realised that The Scalp was the main problem preventing the good drainage of a great area of land. They had refused to join with Boston Corporation in the cost of these first three schemes as they did not solve the Scalp problem.

The silting up of the Scalp section became worse. 1868 was a drought year and there was one day in October that the tide did not reach the Town Bridge in Boston. Vessels of too large a draught to sail up the river now frequently unloaded their cargoes at the mooring points on the Scalp.

Wheeler was of the view that the reclamation of 2000 acres of Kirton and Frampton Marshes in 1870 had made the problem worse. These marshes used to be covered to a depth of two feet of water at high tide and he argued that this work had greatly reduced the volume of tidal water daily scouring the river channel through the Scalp.

A series of nine wet years from 1875 to 1883 caused continuous and serious floods in the catchment area inland. Farmers suffered heavy losses and in some cases ruin. This convinced the Drainage Commissioners that the outfalls of all the main drains needed to be improved. Thomas Garfit MP was influential in persuading them to adopt the 'cutting through the clays' scheme. £161,000 was to be raised, mainly from the drainage commissioners and was apportioned as follows: The Witham General Commissioners, £37,000; the Fourth District, £49,000; the Black Sluice, £65,000; and the Corporation of Boston, £10,000. In the event this was more than enough.

J. E. Williams was appointed Chief Engineer and the work commenced in 1880. At the same time work commenced on the dock in Boston and this was opened in 1884. When all the work was finished in 1887 Mr. Williams was able to report with great satisfaction to the Witham Outfall Board as follows:-

Gentlemen, it affords me pleasure to report that the Works authorised under the Witham Outfall Improvement Act are now completed. The most important section of these Works was, as you are aware, the forming of the new Outfall Channel between Hobhole Sluice and Clayhole in the Estuary of the Wash, a work locally known as the cut through the clays.

The first sod of this new channel was cut on the 14th December, 1880, and the work within the shelter of the tidal embankments was carried on by means of three powerful navvies, eight locomotives, and numerous barrow and wagon roads, whilst the exposed or extreme ends of the channel were excavated by dredging.

The total length of the new channel is 3 miles, or fully a mile and a half less than the old circuitous channel through the shifting sands (at the Scalp). The total quantity of the excavations was nearly 2,000,000 cubic yards, and as a further illustration of the magnitude of the work, I may mention that its sectional capacity (27ft deep, 130ft bottom, 400ft width, at high tide) is in excess of that of either the Suez Canal or the Amsterdam Ship Canal.

The first vessel passed through the new channel on April 7th, 1884, and the permanent closing of the old channel was then actively proceeded with. To effect this it was necessary to form a tidal embankment of great stability, about half a mile in length, across the old channel below Hobhole Sluice. Owing to

GENERAL PLAN
Williams 1887 Article

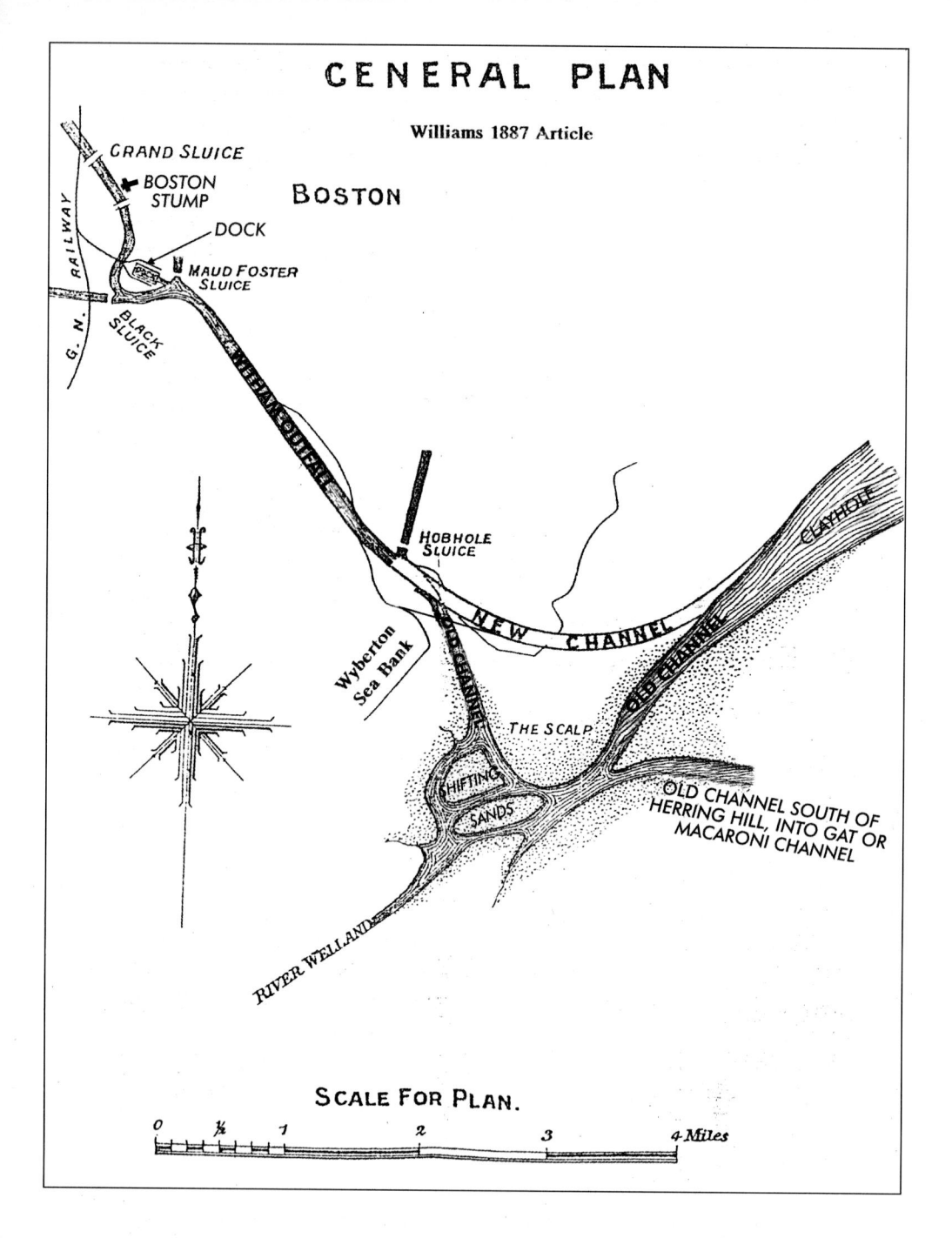

the rapid rise and velocity of the tidal waters in the old channel at this point, its final closing was a most difficult element in the scheme. The work was, however, successfully accomplished on the 20th August, 1884.

The work has already increased the navigable capacity of the Port of Boston from vessels of 300 tons to 2000 tons. The works have in short increased the navigable depth eight feet and adapted the river to the modern class of shipping. The old sills of the Grand Sluice became bare at low water for the first time on the 4th May, 1886, and the absolute gain or depression already acquired in the low water level at the Sluice is 4 feet. The total area draining into the Witham Outfall is about 762,215 acres but of this area only 194,649 acres contribute towards the cost of the improvement and maintenance of the outfall, the total expenditure upon which, to date, including Parliamentary expenses and Land, is £167,941. 7s. 7d.

The large depression in the outfall is in excess of my anticipation, being 5ft 6in at the Hobhole and 4ft at the Grand Sluice. It practically means the raising of the fen lands by this amount.
Your obedient servant,
John Evelyn Williams M. Inst. C.E., May 21st, 1887

Thus concluded an immense engineering project which had taken 90 years to plan and complete. It exceeded the strategic aims outlined by Rennie. In particular it solved the 'silting up' problems of the Haven and produced a self-scouring channel which, even in 1999, requires little attention or cost to maintain.

The first ship to sail up the new channel and into the newly constructed Boston Dock was the 1700 ton Myrtle on Sunday 20th December 1884, with a cargo of cotton seed.

Some of the details and human stories of this great effort are to be found in contemporary newspaper articles.

200 Bankers Loiter in Boston April 14, 1829

The extensive works carrying on for improving the navigation of Boston Haven are proceeding with rapidity; about 200 labouring bankers are employed on the work, and their task is dreadfully laborious, but, judging from their gigantic proportions, as they loiter about the street of this town we should guess they were fully adequate in the undertaking. From this community, there is much reason for believing, many gangs of dangerous robbers have issued whose proceedings have alarmed the country.   And we do think that infinite credit is due to the highly respectable Magistracy of this town and vicinity, and the active police, for preventing any serious robberies at Boston.

The Great Wyberton Bend Soon To Be Cut Off April 28, 1829

During the winter months, the bankers employed on the new line of works for improving the outfall of the haven, have made rapid, indeed almost incredible progress. The new river, it appears, is to commence a short distance on the Boston side of Hobhole, and will proceed in a precisely straight line to the point which juts out from Corporation Marsh, a distance of about a mile and a half. The great evils of the old river have been its huge width, and serpentine course, both of which will be avoided in the new cut; and as it appears to us, much benefit must inevitably result. About half a mile of the new river has already been completed, through marsh land; and now it only remains to fence in the old river, by proper embankments; and when this is completed, certainly one of the most desirable measures ever devised for improving the trade of this town will be accomplished.

Boston Haven July 7 1829

The improvements designed in the outfall of this river are now rapidly advancing towards completion, and a number of the bankers have been discharged. The tide flows rapidly up the new cut, and a bank is being erected from the point where the cut commences, in a line to the opposite shore; the old river is gradually silting up, and the large tract of land thus redeemed will be very valuable.

Shocking Accident September 15 1829

A shocking accident occurred last evening at the new river, near the Scalp, a few miles below this town. One of the bankers, named Martin Duckworth, was on board a lighter, at work, when the tide came in very forcibly; in arranging some ropes in the vessel, one of them, a new cable, was twisted round the poor fellow's leg and before he had time to extricate himself, the flood drove the vessel on with such powerful velocity as actually to sever the bones of his leg just above the ankle. The foot and the connecting part of the limb immediately fell overboard, and the agonized sufferer, fainting from intense pain and loss of blood, also fell into the water. He sunk twice, but rose again, and some of his companions immediately hastened to rescue his maimed body from a watery grave, and to afford him that assistance which he so truly required. They directly formed a litter, upon which a number of them bore him to Boston, a distance of about three miles, the stump of his leg bleeding profusely all the way. About half past six o'clock he was brought past our office and his countenance was then of the most ghastly description; indeed death appeared to have terminated his sufferings. Upon the same litter, several portions of his splintered leg were carried, and altogether the sight was truly horrid. He was promptly attended by Messrs. Snaith and Tuxford, surgeons who shortly afterwards amputated the leg immediately below the knee joint. Up to the period of our going to press this morning, the man was pronounced in a dangerous state.

The spring tides, this turn, have flowed much higher than usual, and the Haven below Boston, at full tide, has consequently presented a very beautiful appearance. Yesterday morning the tide so far overstepped its boundaries, as to flood some of the streets in this town; Wormgate especially was impassable for nearly an hour, unless the person chose to wade knee-deep in water.

Crippled Banker September 22 1829

The labouring banker, whose shocking accident we last week recorded, is now considered out of danger, and likely to recover, though he will of course be crippled for the remainder of his life by the loss of his leg. We are sorry to add that some wretches have been collecting money in his name from the charitable, and absconded with their ill-got pelf. The circumstances of the sufferer are described to be very bad, and hence his poverty adds another pang to his sufferings.

A Banker Fatally Wounded October 6 1829

Martin Duckworth, the banker, who was so horribly mutilated a few weeks since near the Scalp, died at his residence in the parish of Skirbeck last Saturday morning. The poor fellow, some time after he suffered the amputation of his limb, was attacked with intermittent fever, and having been accustomed to injure his constitution by habits of intemperance, his frame could not endure the accumulation of disease, and death terminated his sufferings. He was 38 years old. Upwards of 100 of the bankers attended at his funeral yesterday, each decorated with white cockades; and they conducted themselves with the greatest propriety. Tracts on the solemn subject of death were delivered to them at the grave.

Old River Course Blocked November 10, 1829

On Thursday last the bank which forms the Western boundary of the new line of river from this port to the Scalp was finished. The tide was now been blocked from running in its old course for some months, and the track is rapidly warping up. The immense advantages obtained by the new cut must be evident to the most casual observer; indeed had not this work been completed it would have been impossible to have carried on the vast traffic which has lately prevailed between this town and London.

New River Course at Wyberton Bend November 17, 1829

As we last week briefly notified, the new bank which now forms the Western boundary of Boston river, at its outfall into the sea, has been so far completed as to be open to the public, and a finer piece of work than it is, together with the beautiful stream of water which it so proudly overlooks, is perhaps not to be seen in this part of the country. Instead of, as formerly, a shallow and narrow channel, through which a nearly exhausted ebb crept lazily along, we now have a bold, straight, and rapid river, navigable at all times, and presenting advantages of a superior description. A trifling distance beyond this, the old river suddenly merged considerably to the right, and after describing nearly a circle of about a mile, again came into its natural course, a very little way below the spot where it deviated. And here the grand object of the late improvement has been affected, for a new cut is made in a straight line narrowing the outfall very materially, and thus securing a rapidity of current which is observable through the whole distance from hence to the flood-gates at Boston. This being completed, the next object naturally was to stop the tide way up the old river, and in order to effect such a necessary object, a strong bank was thrown across the old river in a line with the new cut; this bank, as before intimated, has been now completed, and forms a delightful promenade of about half a mile in length, at the foot of which the river glides by in its course to the sea; on the one hand the mighty ocean is stretched forth to the view, with its ever varying aspect; on the other side is seen the town of Boston, in fine perspective, with the old church proudly prominent in the view. But the great benefits derived from the work are that vessels can now freely pass without delay; and the river is kept perfectly clear from shoals, by the current being accelerated so materially in consequence of the channel being narrowed. Thus the natural deposit of the sea is carried back by the ebb, but meeting with the flood it is forced into the old channel, which is as yet left open at the side next the sea; there the water is allowed to deposit the alluvial matter, and the consequence already is that the land thus redeemed, to the extend of several hundreds of acres, is now nearly as high as the neighbouring pastures. To more fully illustrate the subject, we may add that from Boston harbour to the Scalp we did not observe a single vessel which had been stopped for want of water to proceed in its voyage. There were several vessels, certainly at anchor off the Scalp, but they were either waiting a return of more favourable wind, or of tide, to waft them on their various courses; we sincerely hope that the measure thus taken will fully redeem the port; but cannot however, close this article without remarking that captious persons may be found to object even to this improvement. The idle sailor would rather prolong his voyage, the hauler would not care how difficult it was to sail down the river, but these must give way to the public good.

Removing a Locomotive March 16, 1881

Some time ago the contractors for the New cut had considerable difficulty in taking two locomotives from the railway, over the Grand Sluice, and on to the New Cut. At that time the ground was in a very slippery condition. On Monday they had a task almost as difficult. A new locomotive, also destined for the works, arrived at Boston Station and preparations were made for its removal from the railway waggon to a dray, near the passenger station. This occupied a considerable time, and when the removal was accomplished, the weight of the engine caused the dray to sink into the ground. All efforts to remove it proved unsuccessful, and eventually the aid of a traction engine and about a score of horses had to be obtained in order to pull the dray and its burden into West-street. It was then taken down West-street road, Carlton-road and Fydell-street. Considerable difficulty was experienced in getting it over the steep ascent of the Sluice Bridge, but after that obstacle had been surmounted it was speedily removed to the works. The operations at the Station were witnessed by a large crowd of people and we understand there are six other locomotives to follow.

Chaplain for the New Cut

We are informed that the Witham Outfall Board, at a meeting to be held on Wednesday next, will consider the advisability of having a chaplain to hold religious services amongst the navvies during the procedure of the work. It is possible that, with all the clergymen we have in Boston and the neighbourhood; with so many Nonconformist and local preachers; and with a captain and two lieutenants of the "Salvation Army" in our midst, the spiritual condition of the navvies at the new cut has so far been a matter of indifference to them all? If so, we suggest that the last new comers – the Salvation Army – should migrate at once to the Scalp, where we feel sure the county magistrates would not prevent them singing on Sundays or any other days.

Coals for the New Cut

When the contractors for this work get the whole of their engines at work we understand they will require about 100 tons of coals per week; and the contract of Mr. James Wood, coal merchant, of Boston, to supply the same, has been accepted.

The Progress of the Outfall June 3, 1882

The rapid progress being made with the Dock Works will naturally cause more attention to be paid to the improvement of the outfall, and the probable advancement and completion thereof. Indeed, it is that the Boston dock will be completed, if not prior to the outfall, simultaneous therewith; and the important bearing which the outfall works have upon the successful working of the dock will naturally cause some anxiety to see the cut through the clays completed.

On Wednesday, an ordinary meeting of the River Witham Outfall Board was held at the Central Room of the Guildhall, Boston. Prior to the meeting the works at the outfall were inspected. Three steam navvies were at work at the end of the cut, the natural bank of the river which crosses the outfall at this particular point having been reached. The ballast trucks, after being filled by the navvies, are taken back to the nearest slope and drawn to the top of the bank. A locomotive conveys them along the newly constructed embankment towards the sea where each truck is taken separately by another engine to the extremity of the embankment, and its contents emptied out so as to add to the length of the bank. This process is continually going on at both sides. A cross bank has been built below the extremity of the marsh, and this was completed on Tuesday shutting out the waters from the second section of the cut until the required depth is obtained at this part, and the banks properly secured. Beyond this cross bank the excavation must be done at low water, or by dredging only. The dredger is now employed at the point where the old channel of the river communicates with the New Cut, but so far it has done very little work. Preparations are being made for closing up the old channel. Already a portion of the new embankment has been built from the new cut side; and the foundation of the embankment on the opposite side is being prepared. It will be necessary to close up the old channel entirely before the new one is opened; and, as this will have to be done for the most part at a single tide, the work will be very difficult indeed. A number of old barges, smacks, etc. are being obtained to sink across the mouth of the channel at this point and form the basis of the embankment. Several loads of sleepers are being taken down for use in this way also. The work as a whole is progressing more rapidly than it was sometime ago, but it is not nearly half completed yet according to the calculations of the engineers.

Visit of the Outfall Works July 29, 1882

On Thursday a large party of gentlemen from Boston and the neighbourhood paid a visit to the Outfall Works to inspect the progress of the same and afterwards dined at the Milk House Hotel. A brief account of the present state of the works as seen on Thursday may be of interest to our readers. The cut, as is generally known, passes through a clay marsh extending from the Scalp to Clay Hole. The

A Ruston steam navvy

work was naturally divided into two parts by the bank of the river which crossed the Cut about at its centre the first half of the work is now nearly completed, the material having been used to form the banks all along, and build another cross bank near to the end of the cut, so that it might be worked without interference from the tidal water. The central channel all along is the required depth. Passing on to the second half, the work was found in an advanced stage. About 700 men were busy removing a layer of silt. This has to be completed before the three steam navvies can be again used, as a bed of gravel and shells between the silt and the clay holds a large quantity of water, and causes the two substances to mix together in the process of removal by the steam navvies. Until the silt is removed, the wonderful machines which do so much work will stand idle. The silt, as fast as it is removed, is taken to the summit of the bank by two locomotives and deposited there. It is also being removed by carts, which are each drawn up the bank by three horses. This part of the works had a very animated appearance, as in addition to the process described, men were at work draining, an engine and centrifugal pump removing the surplus water to the marsh outside, and the "teetotal gang" were doing the toughest piece of work in the cut removing clay by a horse plank from the bottom to the summit. Beyond the temporary cross bank, the south bank of the Outfall extends some distance and will have to be formed 400 yards further. The north bank will not extend so far, but it has to be carried some distance further yet. Some idea of the progress of the work may be gathered from the fact that about a million cubic yards of earth have been excavated, and the total quantity estimated for excavation is 1,700,000. When the second part of the cut is completed the cross banks at either end will be removed and the tidal water admitted at the top end in order to flush out the silt at the bottom end. What is not carried out in this way will be dredged. There seems an immense quantity of work to get through yet, but when contrasted with what has already been done, the largest half has evidently been disposed of; but it is questionable whether another year will see the completion of the work. Mr. Monk is now paying about £1000 per week wages. The men who form the teetotal gang earn the most wages and do the most work. They have averaged each man from £2. 2s. to £2. 10s. per week since the commencement of the work, and a finer gang of men could not be seen on the works. The magnitude of the undertaking can now be seen; and it is evidently one of the largest engineering works executed in the county. On Thursday Mr. J. E. Williams, C. E. (Engineer to the Outfall Board), Mr. Monk and Mr. Scott were on the works, and afforded every facility for the inspection.

Concert at the New Cut May 13, 1882

A concert was given in the Mission room at the New Cut on Wednesday evening last by members of the Boston Church Choir. This was one of several free entertainments that have been arranged by Mr. Burton for the navvies engaged at the Outfall works. Judging by the enthusiastic reception of the vocalists, Mr. Burton's efforts are greatly appreciated. The concert passed off well, and was brought to a conclusion by the National Anthem in which the audience joined heartily.

Christmas Tree at the New Cut January 6, 1883

On Monday night a Christmas Tree was held in the Mission room at the Outfall Works. The articles were provided by Mrs. Garnett (of Ripon), and Mrs. Simonds and family (of Fishtoft). The latter ladies were present and rendered invaluable service by superintending the dressing of the tree and afterwards by distributing the various articles, quite 400 in number, which were useful, ornamental and amusing in their character. The Rev. S. Staffurth, vicar of Freiston, who was present, together with his wife, in a well chosen little speech said he could not but feel the contrast between inside and outside the Mission room on that occasion. Outside not only were the roads in a terrible state, and he felt they might be all the better for a good scraping, but it was dark too and he had found himself in many quagmires since he left home.

Floods - Outfall Works Saved March 17, 1883

One of the most disastrous tides on record rose on the East Coast of Lincolnshire on Sunday evening, and in no part of the country was the damage greater than in the neighbourhood of Boston. The streets of the town were flooded, the river banks greatly damaged, houses, granaries and shops under water, and, worst of all, the banks of the Haven gave way in several places flooded from 1000 to 2000 acres of land, and doing damage represented by thousands of pounds.....

Proceeding further on our journey we found that at the Outfall Works, although the previous twenty-four hours had been a time of great anxiety, the water had been prevented from filling the cut, and, in that way doing an enormous amount of damage to the works and entailing a serious loss to the contractor. We learned that, on the previous day the navvies had been busily engaged until five o'clock in the afternoon, strengthening all weak places in the newly-formed bank, (by the advice of Mr. J. E. Williams, M.I.C.E.) and taking every possible precaution to prevent the water of the expected high tide finding its way into the cut. The first engineer, who was to some extent responsible for the safety of the works, went on duty on Saturday night, and never left his post until Monday morning after the tide had got the turn. Here and there the water found small inlets and the spouts of the pumping engines which had not been blocked up in the hurry of taking other precautions proved a means of conducting a good deal of water into the works; and, at the further end, sufficient found its way to stop the two steam navvies and several gangs of men from resuming work on Monday morning. Still the great damage which might have occurred was averted.

A Tea for Navvies November 24, 1883

On Tuesday evening a very interesting tea party took place at the Corn-exchange. About 600 navvies, by the kind invitation of Mr. T. Cheney Garfit, assembled and partook of tea together, and were afterwards entertained by a dissolving view exhibition.

New Channel Open December 8, 1883

The New Outfall Cut, between Hobhole and Clayhole, is now open from end to end.

First Ship in New Channel April 19, 1884

Navigation of the New cut-The first sea-going vessel, viz the ketch Margaret and Maria, 90 tons burthen (in ballast) under the command of Captain Thomas Butler, Spain-place, Boston, passes safely through the New Cut on Monday, April 7th.

Dredging New Channel April 26, 1884

There is still three feet six inches of soil to dredge from the lower end of the New Cut before the channel is completed, but already vessels use the new route whenever the tides serve. On Wednesday a large timber laden ship of 300 tons Count Van Platen, from Memel, with cargo of timber, passed through the cut on her way up the river to Messrs. Lewin and Harrison's timber yard. She drew thirteen feet of water. There was at that time seventeen feet of water in the new channel, although on Wednesday the tides were only half spring tides; so that it is fair to suppose when another 3½ feet of bottom is removed there will be twenty-six feet of water in the channel at spring tides. This will surpass the anticipation of the most sanguine engineers.

How did the Scalp get its name?

Ron Jessop who fished for mussels here for forty years until 1996, latterly on his boat 'Medway Harvest', believes the name is derived from the traditional word for a bed of mussels 'Mussel-Scaup'.

3 steam navvies at outfall works in 1882

Lighting the Navigation Lamps by Richard Austin

The Haven frozen at Hobhole in 1963

Before electricity was used for the purpose, paraffin oil was used as fuel to light the navigation lights along The Haven. They were important, then as now, for a ship's pilot to 'line up on' to judge to centre of the deep water channel. Each light had a small hut at its base into which the lamp could be lowered for refuelling, trimming and lighting. These required daily attention so the Harbour Commissioners built a hut at Cut End to house the person employed for the purpose. This was destroyed by rough seas sometime before 1914 so a boat was firmly moored on the river bank nearby.

Mrs. Tilly Russell recalls visiting it on many occasions as small girl during the First World War, when Teddy Hall lived a very solitary life on board. He was quite a character, she fondly recalls, who entertained his infrequent visitors in his well-kept home by playing a fiddle with a fair degree of skill. Groceries for Teddy were often delivered to their cottage at Frampton Roads and she went on foot with her brothers and sisters to take them to the boat, a round trip of about six miles. From time to time Teddy rowed the eight miles to Boston for his other provisions.

Later Banker Woods recalls that Teddy Myers was employed for the purpose but he cycled daily from Boston to Wyberton Roads and then on to the Cut End down Commissioners Road to perform his important duties.

Floods and Drainage by Stuart Hemmings and Richard Austin

When the highest tides occur most of Wyberton is more than two metres (7 feet) below sea level. It is therefore not surprising that the parish has a long history of flooding and poor drainage.

Today Wyberton is protected by two lines of sea banks and has a central drainage channel the length of the parish known as the 'Towns Drain'. This takes water south-east to the Wyberton Marsh pumping station but some water flows north-west by gravity into the Hammond Beck before being lifted by the Chain Bridge pumps. It was not until these two very powerful electric pumping stations were commissioned in 1966 and 1967 that the citizens of Wyberton could sleep peacefully in times of potential flooding. The Chain Bridge pumps take the water from the west of the A16 and the Marsh pumps to the east. The three 90 hp pumps at Chain Bridge can lift 222 tonnes (222,000 litres) of water per minute the three metres into the South Forty Foot drain. At the other end of the parish the three 100 hp pumps have to lift the drainage water six metres (20 feet) at high tide which they do at the rate of 168 tonnes (168,000 litres) per minute into The Haven.

This secure and happy situation is the result of great toil, struggle and expense over a period of more than 1000 years.

It is far from certain when the medieval sea and river banks were built. The dating of banks currently depends on finding shards of pottery left by the builders or earlier occupants. Unfortunately none have been found to answer this question. The 18th century suggestion that they had Roman origins has been discounted. Evidence from other parishes suggests that they were erected by community effort as early as the ninth century, some time before the Norman Conquest. There are written references to their existence in about 1200. There is also a record at this time of the enclosure of some *Newland* beyond the sea bank near Wyberton Roads.

In about 1170 a major bank-building project was completed at the northern end of the parish to protect Wyberton from flooding from the freshwater fens. This bank is now marked by the Old Hammond Beck and Chain Bridge Roads.

The first banks were far from secure. Major flooding had been a recurring problem until the double bank system and associated enclosures were completed in the last century. There is now a proposal to abandon the outer bank in due course. The soggy history of the parish suggests this is a bad idea!

Flooding has been worse at some periods than others; for example in the tenth and eleventh centuries major floods are recorded on about a dozen occasions. The 1287 inundation was a particularly bad one and contemporary records state: *All the whole country in the parts of Holland was for the most part turned into a standing pool, so that an intolerable multitude of men, women and children were overwhelmed with the water, especially in the town of Boston, a great part whereof was destroyed.*

Cleansing of the South Forty Foot drain in 1910. Note the chimneys of the brickworks and fertiliser factory at Hubberts Bridge

The poor state of the sea banks has been a cause for concern many times in the last nine hundred years. On October 5th 1571 there was serious flooding. The Court of Sewers, formed in the reign of King Henry VIII and which was the fore-runner of the present day drainage boards, recorded at that time: *all the fen bankes belongyng to the towne of Wiberton arr in great ruen and decay in dyverse and many places to the great noyans of the countrey for lak of exalting and reparyng of those see bankes.*

The constant possibility of flooding has influenced many things in the parish. It will be noted that the Church and the older houses are built on the highest ground, which can be as much as three feet higher. The prestigious old dwelling sites at Wybert's Castle and Tytton Hall had their own embankments for defence against floods as well as marauders. Grassland is much less affected by flooding than arable crops. This will be one reason why there was so little land cropped until the risk of flooding was negligible.

Before the building of the pumping stations the two oufalls for the Wyberton Towns Drain were sluice gates at Chain Bridge and Slippery Gowt. In 1733 the

Wyberton Marsh Pumping Station

1733 sluice at Slippery Gowt

Keystone on 1733 sluice

Court of Sewers made an order *that the existing sluice at Slippery Gowt should be wholly taken down and rebuilt with brick and timber 38 ft long, 6 ft high and 3 ft 6 ins wide.* The cost was £297. 11s. The work was well done by a builder with the initials T. B. as it remains largely intact and is still in use today. It must surely be the oldest surviving sluice in England.

There was a disastrous flood in 1810 which covered the parish on the evening of Saturday 10th November. 2ft 6in (0.75 m) of water was recorded in the Church when The Haven banks were breached in several places by a particularly high 'eagre' or tidal bore, driven by gale force winds. Many families in Wyberton were left totally ruined. Robert Keall was a farmer at Wyberton Roads who lived and farmed adjacent to the sea bank. He lost all his live- and dead-stock and he and his wife lived in reduced circumstances for the rest of their lives.

As a result of this calamity the residents of the parish decided to significantly increase expenditure to improve the sea bank. In 1811 the rate for sea defences was 2s.1d. per acre. This increased to 16s. per acre in 1815 but then gradually fell until by 1838 it was only 1d. per acre. As well as using silt and clay for improving and raising the bank at this time large quantities of chalk were purchased and brought in by boat. For example, 693 tonnes was acquired between May and August 1822.

In 1841 the big bend in The Haven at Slippery Gowt was straightened. This left the 1733 sluice half a mile from fast tidal water. The channel provided soon silted up, the outfall became useless and all water had to flow the full length of the parish into The Hammond Beck. As a result drainage was much worse. In 1864 the Boston Harbour Commissioners embanked the marsh but refused to provide a sluice through the new bank. The Wyberton Select Vestry mounted legal proceedings to force the issue and won the day. Consequently a new sluice was built into the bank at Slippery Gowt and the connecting drain cleaned out and deepened.

The new sluice however was less well constructed than that of 1733. It was a continual problem and had to be rebuilt several times. For example, on the night of Sunday 17th March 1883 it was badly damaged when the high tide overtopped the bank at Slippery Gowt and breached the bank in several places. Another hazard was that driftwood sometimes prevented the self-closing doors sealing as the tide rose. The Slippery Gowt Sluice was rebuilt for the last time in that year when, during reconstruction work the high spring tide broke through and flooded the land. The Black Sluice IDB accepted some responsibility and the owners, Harold Wrisdale, John and Eliza Tutty and H. White received compensation amounting to £2002. 6s. 7d.

The last breach of the sea bank occurred on the evening of 31st January 1953 when the bank at Wyberton Marsh was overtopped. Mrs. Kathleen Clark remembers returning with her husband to their cottage at Bradley's Farm at about 10 pm. They were amazed to find the dykes full and the moon shining on a sea of water from near their house to the sea bank. Walter Clark was shepherd to Walter Tunnard. He was immediately concerned about the welfare of his flock whose meadow had been inundated. Unmindful of the best suit he was wearing, he went to their rescue and managed to get them out of the water. In the morning they could see that the water had washed down the bank in two or three places. The local farmers and their men all rallied to help and worked desperately to plug the breaches with sand bags to stop the following tides breaking through again.

Until the Black Sluice Internal Drainage Board took over responsibility for parish drains and dykes in 1935 they were maintained under the direction of the parish Dykereeves. They were usually farmers and two were appointed annually by the Select Vestry and, after 1894, by the Parish Council. Their duty was to direct and pay for any work on the banks or parish dykes including the Towns Drain. The parish paid them a small daily allowance plus expenses. In 1835 they received 4s. 8d. per day. They also had to collect a rate from every occupier of land to pay for the work. This was set by The Vestry and they had to present accounts at the end of each year.

Breach at Slippery Gowt 1937

Wildfowling by Alan Day and June Barton

The pursuit of ducks, waders and geese on Wyberton Marsh has a long history both as a source of food and a sport. Today it is an amateur hobby pursued and regulated by the Spalding and District Wildfowling association. Members have a licence to shoot The Scalp between The Old Way and The Haven in season. The RSPB also allow them to shoot on the mud below the high water mark.

Flight nets, muzzle loaders and punt guns have been used in the past with varying effect. The origins of the sport go back to local inhabitants known as 'Fen Slodgers' who, before the nineteenth century, made part of their living by netting and shooting birds in the inland Great Fen. They thwarted various proposals and attempts to reclaim this area for almost 200 years by riots in Boston and the destruction of sluices and ditches. However the Great Fen was eventually drained and enclosed in the 1790's and they were forced to rely on the salt marsh.

Before effective shotguns became available in about 1800, birds were caught in nets. In 1554 Harry Albyn owned a *fowlying neytte* with rope valued at two shillings. Again in 1581 William Rollinson listed *fowling gears* amongst his possessions. By Victorian times large nets six foot high and up to a quarter of a mile long were being deployed on the outmarsh. They were made of twine with a 5-7 inch mesh. The best catches were usually made on moonless nights in November when the migrant birds arrived. Widgeon, curlew, knot and plover were all caught and usually sold by the dozen. Large flocks of geese and duck often burst through and broke down the netting. Eggs were also collected in the nesting season.

The first positive indication that shotguns were being used in the Parish is in 1669 when Richard Ringstead had *utenssills about shot makinge* valued at £2, which was worth about the same as a cow at that time. These first shotguns were muzzle-loaded. They were slow and awkward to handle. They also required time to recharge and were usually only effective against birds at rest, hence the term 'a sitting duck'. It was not until the advent of the breech-loading cartridge gun about 100 years ago that matters improved.

Up to the Second World War the punt gun was used widely for commercial gain in the creeks and on the edge of the marsh. Waples Hall was the last wildfowler to practice the art on this marsh. He lived in a cottage behind the bank of Kirton Marsh and the creek running out from there is still known as 'Halls' creek'. He would lie low in the punt in a creek such as this and wait for a raft of duck to float upstream on the rising

A 2-man punt gun by C.W. Pilcher

tide. When they were in range of the gun he would alert them and fire into the mass as they lifted off the water. Timing had to be perfect as the gun was fixed to the centre line of the punt, which was eased through the freezing water by the gunner lying prone using hand-held wooden paddles. The birds were collected and wounded ones dispatched with a 'cripple stopper', which was a shoulder gun carried in the punt. The muzzle-loaded punt gun was then recharged but very often would only be fired once in an outing.

These duck were mainly widgeon. They were often worth a useful 5 shillings per couple and were sent by the sackful to London on the train.

During the last war wildfowling was difficult as the Marsh was officially off-limits and cartridges were scarce. However meat was rationed so the few who were able to gain access did well. After 1945 more people had shotguns. These 'shoulder gunners' disturbed the rafts of duck, and a state of near anarchy began to develop. Birds were fired at out of range, five-shot automatic shotguns and even rifles were illegally used. Also farmers' nearby land was poached for pheasant and rabbit. It was not until the farmers, the South Lincolnshire Wildfowlers and the Wash Group got together that order was restored, with proper membership and control of the access points.

The Pick-up - Waples Hall

The Shot - Waples Hall

A Day out on Wyberton Marsh by Alison Austin

For the first half of this century going "down the Marsh" was a popular pastime for people of all ages from Boston and the villages to the south. The road past the Moores Arms lead to Frampton Marsh or you could go down Streetway. In the 1920's and 30's, between the Wars, when the seaside at Skegness or Hunstanton was too far away for a day's outing, young people and whole families would go down on to the Marsh and picnic. Many people bicycled down and left their cycles at the end by the Sea Bank but cars were left halfway down the track if you went along the road through Frampton. Early this century the Marsh was the destination for Sunday School outings and "The Pincushion" and "the Hammer and Pincers" would take it in turns to provide refreshments.

There were three huts on the bank, to the right of the road was one belonging to the Tunnard family and to the left were two more. The Caswells had a hut on wheels that had formerly been the sort used when cultivating by traction engine and the Fossitts had one called "Hyperion" after a racehorse. Further along to the left Nurse "Dicky" Black had her hut, set just below the top of the bank and facing the outmarsh. It was made of corrugated iron painted green and lined with wood.

The Gulch creek 1929

Bathing belles on the marsh c.1930

The marsh was grazed by sheep and cattle that would be brought over the bank when the tide was high and put into either the "Weekday" field or the "Sunday" field. The grass was criss-crossed with sheep paths but after a high tide these would be muddy.

Opposite Miss Black's hut the roadway lead on to the Marsh and down to the Gulch or Big Creek. In summer people would come down to swim after work but weekends would be family occasions. Usually they would picnic on the bank and then the energetic ones would play rounders on the sand. (There was much more sand in the Gulch Creek than there is nowadays). Girls would tuck their skirts into their knickers and men, often wearing their "Sunday best" would roll up their trouser legs. As the tide came in there was sufficient water in the creek for swimming. People would change in the grass beside the creek. Children would delight in sliding down the steep muddy banks into the water.

Men would take their shrimping nets and the shrimps were boiled up in the hut or taken back home for tea. If you walked further out towards the River Welland men would "butt" prick, which meant stabbing dabs with a fork. Cockles could be gathered from the bed of the creek with a rake and put into a basket on a

Dabbing or 'butt pricking'

pony. On the higher ground beyond the Creek grows Samphire or "sea asparagus" as it is sometimes called. This is another example of the free food that the sea marsh has to offer and one that fetches exorbitant prices in London today.

Mr. Frank Johnson, who lived in "Bottle Hall" in the last enclosure of Frampton, used to sell ice-cream which he collected from Archers of Boston on a bicycle. During the Second World War the Marsh was out of bounds and was taken over by the troops, some of whom were billeted at the Grange in Kirton and some in Boston. Frank would supply them with tobacco and beer and bootlaces and whatever "home comforts" he could get hold of from a little hut directly opposite their mess, alongside the road just below the pillbox on the bank. In fact he also ran a club like a "NAAFI" in the front room of his house and soldiers would come in an evening to drink beer and play darts.

After the War refreshments continued to be served from Nurse Black's hut, now owned by Mrs Colam, and you could buy pop and crisps and fruit from her. Youngsters would camp below the bank in the summer and sit around a campfire in the evening. When the tide was very high the water would reach the steps of the hut. The other huts had disappeared by then.
Swimming and picnicking continued until the late 1950's but the path down to the Gulch became harder to follow after every winter and now it is almost impossible to get right out unless you are prepared to get wet or muddy, although the footpath sign bravely points out towards the sea. Now that the RSPB protects the area, the public is not encouraged to stray far from the bank. Over recent years the whole Marsh has silted up and the water rarely laps the bank as it used to at high tide.

And Nurse Black's hut has vanished; a local farmer bought it and dismantled it.

Cooking Samphire

Wash thoroughly to remove all traces of mud and salt.

To eat fresh, boil or steam for about 10-15 minutes until it comes off the stalk with a fork and serve as a vegetable.

To preserve, blanch or cook and then bottle in vinegar. Keep for several months.

Jenny and Joyce Colam serving refreshments from the hut c.1950

The Marsh Reserves by Tony Smith and Lewis James

A Twite on Wyberton Marsh

The Wash is exceptionally rich in plants, birds and invertebrates. In 1972 it was declared a site of Special Scientific Interest by the Nature Conservancy Council, now called English Nature. More recently the international importance of The Wash was recognised by designating it as a Ramsar Site and a Special Protection Area.

In 1976 the Lincolnshire Trust for Nature Conservation acquired 171 hectares of that part of Wyberton Marsh known as The Scalp. Later in the mid 1980's the RSPB took over the ownership and management of a further 370 hectares. Although much of this area lies in Wyberton it is commonly known as The Frampton Marsh Reserve.

Redshank nest here at a higher density than anywhere else in Britain. Their beautiful piping song can be heard in the spring and summer as they hang in mid-air on quivering wings.

It is in the winter that the Wash provides a truly outstanding wildlife spectacle, with over 300,000 wading birds, ducks and geese.

Many of these can be seen from the sea wall at high tide. Brent geese are particularly conspicuous, with flocks of over 2,000 often present. Hen harriers, merlin and short-eared owls hunt over the Marsh during the day and gather to roost at night. Flocks of twite and Lapland bunting can be found feeding on the seeds of saltmarsh plants.

The Marsh plants are at their best in late summer when the colourful sea aster and sea lavender are in flower. Samphire is common on the saltmarsh edge. Its fleshy green spikes were once often used in the manufacture of glass, hence its name, glasswort. It is traditionally picked by local people for eating either lightly boiled or pickled.

The RSPB manages the reserve by low density summer grazing with cattle which maintains suitable vegetation structure for nesting redshank and wintering brent geese. This also helps to retain livestock farming in the area which benefits a range of farmland birds and other wildlife.

Redshank by Neil Smith

Wyberton Park

People and Places

Ralphs Lane Gibbet - The fate of a murderer by Hilary Healey

Ralphs Lane, which joins the 'old main road' by the Blacksmith's shop, was formerly just regarded as the Donington Road. It acquired its present name from Ralph Smith, whose corpse was exhibited on a gibbet some 500m down this road, just over the parish boundary in Frampton. The site is marked by a small commemorative plaque.

Ralph Smith in gibbet by Hilary Healey

Ralph Smith of Wyberton was executed on May 16th 1792 for the murder of Gentle Sutton on 1st February of that year. Sutton lived in a cottage described much later as being *halfway between Frampton House and the 'new Church'* (i.e. St. Michael's Church, not built until 1863), *at Frampton West End.* Sutton's son was named in the newspapers as Vear, and there is a house called Vere Cottage at that location on Bannisters Lane, Frampton. The different spelling of Vere may not be significant. Sutton was killed by hammer blows to the head, and the murderer had even replaced the hat with some of his victim's brains in it! Clothes and some silver teaspoons were stolen, and the theft, combined with the word of a young witness, secured Smith's conviction. He was alleged to have sold the goods to a pub landlord in Fiskerton, near Lincoln. Smith was also said to have borne a grudge against Sutton, but this cannot be verified.

Ralph Smith had perviously been given a transportation sentence, though it was never actually carried out. He probably did his time on the notorious 'hulks' or prison ships. In some, but not all, accounts he protested his innocence throughout. When measured up by a Boston Blacksmith (possibly named Clarkson) for the 'chains', the iron cage in which his body was to be encased, he was especially distressed, as he said it was not part of the sentence. No doubt he was afraid at the thought of not having a proper burial. This grisly display of the body, the gibbeting, was apparently done at the request of *certain persons in the neighbourhood*. Nationally this was actually a short-lived practice and ceased in 1835. Smith was executed at Lincoln Castle and the body brought back by cart, attended by the under-Sheriff of Lincolnshire. A great crowd of people came to see the sight, the place being *exceedingly lively, especially on Sundays when it was more like a fair*. It is not known for how long a body was hung up, but the remains would be buried nearby. Often such sites are on a parish boundary, but this was no doubt the nearest piece of waste ground in this case.

As always, people took parts of the gibbet (and even, we are told, of the skeleton!) away as souvenirs. Part of the oak post was made into a tobacco bowl, still in Boston's Guildhall Museum. It seems that even two hundred years ago the ghoulish public interest in murder and murderers was just as great as it seems to be today.

The Murder of a Policeman by Steve Vessey

In 1847 the Lincolnshire Constabulary was formed. The area around Boston was supervised by Superintendent Thomas Manton who worked from a newly built police station at Skirbeck Quarter. One of Superintendent Manton's police constables was Alexander McBrian, an Irishman, who had formerly been a Parish Constable at Coningsby.

At 1am on Thursday 25th October 1860, Constable McBrian was patrolling on foot in the Parish of Wyberton. In 1860, a constable's hours of duty were long and it is probable that McBrian had walked from Skirbeck Quarter to Fosdyke earlier in the evening, and at 1am was on his way back to his station. It was a brilliant, moonlit night when a cross-country walk would have presented little problem. McBrian was using the public footpath from Frampton to Wyberton which passes through the east end of Wyberton churchyard. As he entered the churchyard he met a man carrying a shotgun. He hailed the man and asked him what he was carrying the gun for. The man did not reply, but turned towards the Constable and fired the gun, hitting him in the chest and upper right arm. The assailant made off, and the wounded Constable went to the nearby house of Farmer John King for help. King was so drunk that he could not help, so McBrian walked to the rectory, where he roused the Rev. Charles Moore. Mrs Moore gave him some brandy and water, and the Rev. Moore's servant took him to the Skirbeck Quarter Police Station by pony and trap.

McBrian was received by Superintendent Manton who arranged for Doctor Young to attend and treat the injury. In spite of the attention of Doctor Young, and Doctor Adam, and Mr. Broadbent (a Lincoln Surgeon) during the coming days, McBrian grew progressively weaker.

With the arrival of daylight, Superintendent Manton and Sergeant John Coddington commenced enquiries. When they visited the scene of the crime in Wyberton churchyard, they found and preserved some pieces of newspaper which appeared to have been used as wadding in a muzzle-loading gun.

The suspicions of the police then fell on Thomas Richardson and James Burrell, both farm labourers who lived in semi-detached cottages and who worked for John King, the farmer mentioned earlier. Enquiries revealed that King, Richardson and Burrell had been drinking together in the Crown and Anchor

The shooting of PC McBrian by Margaret Cowe

public house at Skirbeck Quarter during the evening before the shooting. The drinking was associated with a "free and easy" provided by a political party in connection with the selection of a new candidate to replace Herbert Ingram M.P. who had recently been drowned. Drink was provided free of charge and it seems that the three men drank liberally. Thomas Richardson, who originally came from Stixwould, had a reputation as a poacher, and had previously threatened to kill police officers who interfered with his nocturnal activities.

Superintendent Manton visited the homes of Richardson and Burrell, and in Richardson's house they found a double-barrelled, muzzle-loading shotgun, of which one barrel was still loaded. Because they were unable to unload the gun, Sergeant Coddington fired it off. After firing, the two officers recovered some more newspaper wadding, which seemed to correspond with that which they had recovered in the churchyard. In Richardson's house they also found his shot-bag (from which he habitually loaded his gun) which contained a mixture of numbers 3, 4 and 6 shot.

On Wednesday 31st October Thomas Richardson was taken to McBrian's bedside at Skirbeck Quarter where, in the presence of a Magistrate, the Constable identified Richardson as the man who shot him. On Thursday 1st November, the Doctors were of the opinion that McBrian would die shortly. Superintendent Manton told his Constable that he was dying and asked him to identify the man who shot him in a "dying declaration". He again identified Thomas Richardson as the man who shot him. McBrian died later that day.

Shotgun pellets taken from the body during a post-mortem examination, and those recovered from the Constable's uniform, were found to be a mixture of 3, 4 and 6 shot. Joseph Towl, a local gunsmith, was of the opinion that such a mixture was very unusual. It was common to mix 3 and 4 shot together, but not to mix 6 shot with it.

The newspaper wadding recovered from the scene and that from Richardson's gun was examined by Captain Philip Bicknell, the Chief Constable of Lincolnshire, who found that both pieces of paper came from the 9th and 10th pages of the Times newspaper of 27th March 1854. Mr. Thomas Cope, the publisher of the Times, also examined the pieces of paper and confirmed that they all came from the same issue of his newspaper.

Constable Alexander McBrian was buried in Skirbeck churchyard on 3rd November. The North Holland Magistrates and the Chief Constable opened a fund for the relief of his widow and family.

A series of inquests were held into the death, and at that time committal proceedings were taken against Thomas Richardson for the murder of Constable McBrian. The inquest verdict was one of *Wilful Murder - against Thomas Richardson*. Richardson was committed for trial at the Lincolnshire Assizes on 8th December.

At the Assize hearing before Justice Baron Bramwell, Messrs. Stephen and Huish represented the prosecution and Richardson was defended by Mr. O'Brian. After a day-long hearing, during which some 16 witnesses were heard, the jury found Thomas Richardson guilty of murder and Baron Bramwell sentenced him to death by hanging. The most important evidence at the trial was that given in relation to the newspaper used as wadding, the unusual mixture of shot sizes from the prisoner's bag and from the wound, and the identification of the prisoner by Constable McBrian in the presence of a Magistrate.

Richardson was held at Lincoln Prison awaiting execution set for 21st December. The police, however, were not popular in 1860, and a petition was organised in Boston for the sentence of death against Richardson to be commuted to one of penal servitude for life. There may also have been a political motive since farmer John King, Richardson's brother-in-law, was a voter, whose vote had been solicited during the drinking session at the Crown and Anchor. The petition was signed by more than 1,000 people, including the Boston and Holland Magistrates. It was accompanied by a note from Rev. Wright Shovelton, a Methodist Minister, to whom Richardson had admitted his guilt when he visited him in prison.

On 19th December 1860, a letter was received at Lincoln Prison, from the Home Office, to the effect that the death sentence against Richardson had been commuted to penal servitude for life.

On 17th January 1861 Richardson was transferred from Lincoln to Wakefield Jail to begin his life sentence.

The Hammer and Pincers by Richard and Alison Austin

The house which is now The Hammer and Pincers, was built by Abraham Faulkner in 1826 alongside the 'Swineshead Ramper' near the Chain Bridge. The Ramper was then a Turnpike Road used by the stage coaches going towards Sleaford and Grantham, and is thought to have been called Sleaford Road.

The house was bought by John Jackson in 1830 who then developed a blacksmith's business. In the 1851 census he is described as a blacksmith and beer seller but the first record of the name 'Hammer and Pincers' is in 1875 when it was conveyed to Alfred Jackson. Alfred's immaculate school arithmetic exercise book, written when he was 12, has been handed down in the Jackson family. They also have an account book in the same elegant style which shows that in 1877 Alfred consistently sold about 400 pints of beer per week. This was purchased from The Robin Hood Brewery in Boston.

He died in 1907 and the blacksmith's shop closed but his widow kept on the licence until she died in 1917. Their son, Walter Jackson, continued as licencee until 1938 although for a seven year period from 1922 to 1929 the pub was closed. The Hammer and Pincers was purchased by Soames and Company (Brewers) in 1929 and now is owned by Tetleys.

Hammer & Pincers c.1938

Hammer & Pincers c.1890

Hammer & Pincers 1999

The Pincushion and the Pinfold by Alison and Richard Austin

The Pincushion Inn or 'Pin', as it is often called, seems to be one of the few pubs of this name in the Country. The exact date of the original part of the building is not known. However the brickwork suggests that it is late eighteenth century and it is shown on the enclosure map of 1795. As the Turnpike Road alongside was constructed about 1780 it is reasonable to assume that it was constructed between those two dates. An early record of the name is in the Parish Poor Book when there is an item:

Sept 15th 1809: For procuring a nurse for a sick man at The Pincushion 2s. 6d.

It is most probable that it took its name from the other 'Pin' next door. This was the village Pinfold, which used to hold stray animals until they were claimed and a fee paid. This compound was fenced with wooden stakes and rails and was almost certainly sited where 287 London Road, Bramley Garden Farmhouse, now stands. The Pinfold had been a village 'institution' for many centuries before the Pincushion was built and there are several references to it in the parish records.

In June 1817 the Vestry ordered that John Ablewhite of Boston was to be paid for repairing the Pinfold and John Hopkins and Saul Tibbs were sworn in as Pinders for the parish that year.
On 21st May 1818 *it was agreed that Wm Webster shall substantially repair the Pinfold with oak posts and fir railing, after which it is to be valued and the Parish pay half the expense. The aforesaid Wm Webster is to keep the key and receive the poundage and to keep the pinfold in proper repair. The surveyor of the Highways is to see that the pinfold is kept in proper repair.*

With the decline in livestock in Wyberton it ceased to be used and in 1878 there is an entry in the minute book of 2nd April:
The materials of the pinfold near the Pincushion to be offered for sale in the Pincushion at the earliest convenience.

The Pincushion has flourished as a Public House. In 1920, when Fanny Meggot was the landlady, a gentleman drove over from Nottingham in his three-wheeler car for a week's holiday. He stayed at the Pincushion for 2s. 6d. per day and spent his time fishing on the South Forty Foot Drain!

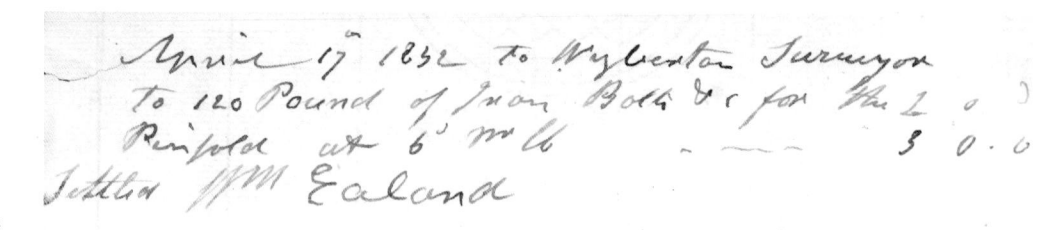

Bill for the repair of the pinfold 1832

Pincushion c.1900

Pincushion 1908

Landlady Fanny Meggot and a visitor's car 1920

The blue period c.1970

Winter 1986

95

Wyberton Park by Colin Cullimore

Despite the name, Wyberton Park was the old rectory for the parish. The original building was a mud and stud structure with carp ponds and an ice house.

In 1687 the incumbent was granted a faculty to rebuild *in brick, and tiled after a more curious and commendable manner, with kitchen, parlour, a large staircase in the midst at the entrance, two chambers, a large study and garrets and a large porch.*

The work was actually completed in 1689, although the large porch was never built. At that time the incumbent, with considerable glebe acreage, was a significant farmer. In 1761 Dr. John Shaw, the Rector, had the North front of the house built. At the same time and in the same style he rebuilt St. Leodegar's chancel as the Early English one was in danger of collapse.

The architect was William Sands Junior of Spalding, also responsible for Fydell House in Boston. It is his typical style with 7 bays, 2 storeys and stone quoins with a pediment breaking from the parapet. The windows have stone surrounds and Dr. Shaw's sons' names, T. Burton Shaw and Edward Shaw, are inscribed on the angle stones.

The old entrance was on the West front with a fine doorcase and carved frieze matching the chimneypiece in the William and Mary main bedchamber. The new entrance on the North front has full Roman Doric engaged columns and a triangular pediment.

Inside there is fine plasterwork, particularly the Roccoco library ceiling and the panelled drawing room ceiling, both thought to be by Edward Goudge who was the plasterer who did the ceilings at Belton House. However it has been suggested that the work was done by an itinerant Italian who worked for James Wyatt when he carried out the neo-classical facelift there and created ceilings in the style of Goudge.

The original 1689 stairs were remodelled and are similar to those at Fydell House and Frampton Hall with 3 balusters per tread alternately turned, twisted and fluted. They are lit by a spacious window in the East wall where the original wall was faced with Georgian brick capped with a moulded cornice.

With the removal of glebe land from the incumbent, the Rectory became a burden and too large for modern requirements. During the 1939-45 war the Church Commissioners made the property available to the Women's Land Army and today ladies, who were in their late teens and early twenties at that time, revisit the house and tell of walking down the Low Road into Boston for Saturday night dances with the soldiers and airmen stationed nearby.

Wyberton Park and staff 1880

Eventually the deterioration of the property made life a misery for the incumbent and the Diocese built a new Rectory in Church Lane, opposite St. Leodegar's, and put the property on the market in 1952. The farmer who grazed cattle on the land was prepared to purchase the property but had no desire to live in the house. Christopher Blackie, anxious to prevent the building falling into further disrepair, bought the house with eight acres and did a marvellous and painstaking job of restoration.

The Church Commissioners required the name to be changed from the Rectory to Wyberton Park. After living happily in the house the Blackies sold it in 1970 and in the following 21 years there were 7 owners; the only one of any length being Tom Sinclair of the well known local Sinclair McGill Seeds Group.

Wyberton Park became the property of the Royal Bank in 1988 following a mortgage foreclosure and after being empty for some time was beautifully restored over a fifteen month period by H. H. Adkins of Wyberton West Road for Colin and Kathy Cullimore. It was sold to John Studholme in 1999.

It is a Grade 2 starred building.

Ice House

At Wyberton Park there is the remains of a symbol of one time gracious living, an Ice House; one of the few in the United Kingdom.

In 1991 it was examined by Lincolnshire Heritage who concluded that the roof had collapsed some time in the last century and only the floor and lower brick walls remained. Consequently it is impossible to date the construction accurately but certainly it was prior to 1689 as it was in existence at the time of the old mud and stud Rectory which was knocked down then to construct what is now the rear portion of Wyberton Park. At that time old maps show an L-shaped pond of the same size as at present.

The pond was deep at the right angle and even today approaches 20 feet at the point where the ice house is located, and the bank has a gentle slope to the entrance. In winter as ice formed in this corner it was cut and dragged up the slope and lowered into the ice house. It was 14 feet deep with a brick floor and walls. Each cutting of ice was wrapped in straw. At the end of the winter the top layers of ice and straw in this underground cavern helped to insulate the lower layers so that often a winter's supply lasted most of the summer. The ice was used to help preserve food by bringing blocks into the slate shelved store room where fruit, jellies and puddings were laid out and meat and game hung from the iron hooks in the ceiling. It was not used, as some books claim, to ice drinks – a more modern habit!

In some ice houses the roof was brick vaulted and then covered with thatch. The Wyberton Park ice house was round like a large brick well with, it seems, wooden beams and a flat, rather than vaulted, roof. It seems likely that the East, South and West sides were covered in earth but the North opposite the pond was thatched with the entrance at the North-East corner.

The ice house was still in operation after the 1689 house was built and beyond 1761, when the North front was added, as the vaulted store room under the house still exists. Although now bricked up, the original entrance across the pond from the ice house can still be seen. It can also be approached through the wine cellar and the vaulted general food cellar. Even in this underground store with its exceedingly thick walls the ice would have melted very slowly. It is still very cold there, even in summer, and allows champagne and white wine to be served at perfect temperature.

An ice-house

ICE HOUSE AT ASHRIDGE HERTS. LIKE A LARGE WELL COVERED BY A BRICK VAULT, CUT OFF BY VAULTED PASSAGE, AS SECTION AT A, ALL BUILT INTO THE HILLSIDE.

Tytton Hall by J. and E. Watson

The precise origins of Titton Hall (original spelling) remain a mystery. The earliest records of the Tytton family date back to 1488 when Margaret Tytton married John Coppledyke, Squire of Frampton, who was Sheriff of the County. It is supposed that the Tytton name died out as there is no mention of the name in a register of 1538. The Crown and the College of St. Mary Magdalen, Oxford held rights over the Lord of the Manor of Tytton from 1539. It is presumed that the property passed into the Coppledyke family as they appear in the Register of 1552. The Cheyney family lived at Tytton Hall after the Coppledykes but the only record of them is a shield painted on a panel over the Rector's seat in St. Leodegar's Church, Wyberton. There is little recorded of the Hall over the next two hundred years. A map of Wyberton in 1791 shows the Hall partly surrounded by a moat. From the scale it probably extended beyond the present boundaries of the gardens into the adjacent field. This indicates that the site was probably once fortified and protected against flooding by an embankment.

Another one hundred years passes until there is a record of Mr. John Wright-Robinson residing there between 1856 and 1861. In 1878 William Lane-Claypon, a Boston banker, is shown as having bought the property. At this time Tytton Hall is regarded as being a plain farmhouse and Mr. Lane-Claypon enlarged and embellished it. From present knowledge of dating old buildings, the central portion of the Hall with its horse hair and plaster walls and low beamed straw and plaster ceilings would seem to date from the early 18th century. The grander and larger rooms with higher ceilings would certainly fit with the late 19th century additions. It was here that Janet Elizabeth Lane-Claypon was born and educated by a Governess. She was later to become a Doctor and eminent research scientist.

The Hall was then occupied by John Caister, who was in residence in 1900, and two years later by William Tom Horry, a Boston Councillor. He was brewer, keen angler and dog breeder. The Times Newspaper carried articles on his success with his Collie Dogs at the Kennel Club show. An angling trophy "The Squire of Tytton Cup" presented by Tom Horry was named after one of his famous Collie Dogs, "The Squire of Tytton".

The Hall then passed to a farmer, Ernest William Bowser, in 1926. It remained in his family until sold to Brian Eastick, a Property Developer. The Hall was

Tytton Hall c.1960

then split from the outbuildings which were developed into a courtyard of eight individual units and the Hall sold off separately to Mr. J. Jones, another Property Developer. The present owners took over the stewardship of the by now neglected property in 1995. It had been converted to eight flats and was in a state of decline. John Watson and his wife, Elizabeth, Consultants at Boston's Pilgrim Hospital, have gradually brought the Hall back to life. It is now returning to its former glory as an elegant family home.

Janet Elizabeth Lane-Claypon, (Lady Forber), 1877-1967
by Warren Winkelsteiner, Jr. (Berkeley, California)

When Janet Elizabeth Lane-Claypon was one year old, she moved from Boston with her mother and father and older sister into Tytton Hall, the Victorian Mansion which her banker father had created out of an ancient Wyberton farmhouse. There she grew up, having a private tutor, as was frequently the case for upper class women. In 1898, the family moved to Hampstead so that Janet Elizabeth could matriculate at the University of London School of Medicine for Women.

Janet Elizabeth was a brilliant student. She received a B.Sc. in 1902, with first class honours in physiology, and a Doctor of Science in 1905. She was designated a 'University Scholar', received a gold medal, and is memorialized with other outstanding women medical students on a plaque hanging today in London's Royal Free Hospital. In 1902, as a student, she became the first woman to receive a British Medical Association research scholarship. In 1908 she received the prestigious Jenner Research Scholarship of the Lister Institute of Preventive Medicine.

Lane-Claypon's professional accomplishments fall into three categories. Early in her career, while she was still a student, she carried out important laboratory studies of reproductive physiology, biochemistry and microbiology. In the second category, she studied the nutritional value for human babies of mother's milk compared to boiled cow's milk. She also wrote extensively on women's and children's health and welfare. From 1917-1923 she served as Dean of King's College for Women. In the third and final category are her studies of cancer epidemiology carried out in the Ministry of Health between 1923 and 1930. In 1926 she pioneered research into breast cancer, identifying most of the risk factors for that disease which are recognized today.

Other notable events in her professional career included involvement with the Medical Women's Federation and appointment as one of the first female magistrates in 1920.

In 1929, Janet Elizabeth Lane-Claypon married Sir Edward Rodolph Forber, the Deputy Secretary at the Ministry of Health. As a married woman, she could no longer remain in the Civil Service and so she retired. She devoted the rest of her long life to religious pursuits as she and her husband moved from place to place in the south of England. Janet Elizabeth died on 17th July 1967 at the age of 90 years. She is buried by her husband in the parish churchyard of Bishopstone in Sussex.

Editorial note: The author of this article is writing a biography of Janet Elizabeth L-C.

Janet Elizabeth Lane-Claypon

Fred Parkes by Alison Austin

Earlier this century Fred Parkes founded what was to become the largest privately-owned trawler fleet in the world. For several years he lived in Wyberton.

Fred Parkes was born in 1879 near Sleaford and moved to Boston as a young boy where his family lived in impoverished surroundings in Pipe Office Lane.

After leaving elementary school at the age of twelve Fred worked firstly at a local brickyard and then as an apprentice to a chemist before starting to work for Elijah Smith. He was a fish merchant with a shop in Boston and stalls at markets in nearby towns. In time Fred was trusted to attend these markets on his own. At a young age he got in the habit of regularly saving a small amount of money. His next job was as a packer on the fish quay in Boston. His prudent saving paid off when his employer, a Mr. Lammie, died and Fred was able to buy his business.

In 1902 Parkes married Gertrude Bailey, daughter of the owner of the Gallows Mills, demolished when Boston Dock was constructed. He built their first home, Coronation Villa, near the top of Wyberton Low Road. Whilst living here they started to attend Wyberton Church. Mrs. Parkes played the organ while he was a Church Warden and a Sidesman.

His next business venture was when he purchased a 10-acre field close to the river and Coronation Villa and turned it into a salt cod farm, complete with drying racks and a light railway track. Soon he was exporting salted dry cod roe to France as bait for catching sardines. This was brought to an end by the First World War. In 1911 he purchased a 109-acre farm in Skirbeck near the Boston Dock on land that was to become the Boston Golf Course. Later he was to buy more land including 400 acres at Kirton Marsh.

Fred Parkes

After some years at a house on London Road, the family moved in 1912 to what is now known as the Vineries on the Low Road. This was a house with no running water, gas or electricity and without a bathroom. There was a well but in time of drought water had to be obtained from a supply on Rowell Row (now the top of the Wyberton Low Road near London Road). There was a magnificent greenhouse on the side of the house, now recently replaced with a modern conservatory. The house came with a 150-acre farm and had one acre under glass. Flowers and bulbs as well as tomatoes and grapes were grown.

In 1885 the Boston Deep Sea Fishing and Ice Company had been formed by a group of influential business and professional men. The Corporation was to build a fish quay and appropriate storage facilities and in 1886 the first trawlers began to operate out of Boston. All the company's trawlers were given Lincolnshire place names and in 1888 we hear mention of the *Kirton* and the *Wyberton* and also the *Skirbeck* and the *Fishtoft*. For the first few years the company ran at a loss but by the end of the first decade it was returning a modest profit. However before the onset of the First World War it was in financial difficulties. By this time Fred Parkes had his own trawlers and was in direct competition with the Boston Company. In 1919 he was invited to become the Boston Company's manager and a director, and duly sold them his own trawlers.

The Vineries 1938

In order to see through his own ideas on running the company, Parkes gradually bought up shares until he had a controlling holding. He then built up a fleet of steam trawlers which by 1922 numbered 37.

In 1922 on 28th February a boat laden with coal, the ss *Lockwood* ran aground in the Haven. It was re-floated but then re-grounded near the mouth of the river and capsized across it, blocking the main channel. There was a three month delay in the salvaging of this vessel, severely threatening the trade of the Port. It was agreed that the Boston Deep Sea Fishing and Ice Company should raise and salvage the *Lockwood* for a sum of £12 000. This was duly completed in the June of that year. There then followed a lengthy legal dispute between the Harbour Commissioners and the ship's owners and then with the Boston Deep Sea Fishing Company concerning payment for the raising of the *Lockwood,* which was settled out of court in 1923 but which resulted in Mr. Parkes removing half of his trawlers to Fleetwood. It was not long before he relinquished all the company's premises at Boston and transferred his fleet from fishing the North Sea to deeper and more distant waters.

Fred and Gertrude left Wyberton in 1923 and went to live in Blackpool. Fred died in Preston in June 1962 at the age of eighty three.

The Lockwood near Hobhole 1922

Footnote

Some time after the 87-ton *Wyberton* had been sold to a buyer in Shanghai, Fred's son, Sir Basil Parkes, on a visit to the Far East learned of the vessel's fate.

She had left Boston in October 1922 and had battled through heavy seas, arriving in Shanghai three months later. She had never successfully completed another trip and local fishermen became fearful of her because everyone who signed up with her either was killed or lost overboard. Eventually he managed to visit her but sadly by then the *Wyberton* was little more than a heap of rust.

Ernest Bowser - 1887 to 1969

E. W. Bowser lived at Tytton Hall from 1926 to 1955. During his life he created a large farming business, E. W. Bowser and Son Limited, extending to some 2000 acres, as well as being a prominent public figure. In 1943 Mr. Bowser was High Sheriff of Lincolnshire.

For many years he was a magistrate and had a lifelong interest in drainage matters, serving on various drainage authorities from the ages of 31 to 71. He was chairman of the Witham Fourth Internal Drainage Board from 1935 to 1957. Mr. Bowser was also chairman of the Boston NFU for 18 years. During the 1939-45 conflict he was a member of the War Agricultural Executive Committee which had draconian powers to ensure the maximum amount of food was grown in the area.

His ashes are buried in Wyberton churchyard and his farming business is now run by his grandson Robert and his great-grandson Nicolas.

E.W. Bowser
High Sheriff of Lincolnshire 1943

Dickie Dale - Motorcycle Ace by Richard Austin

Between 1951 and 1961 R. H. Dale achieved international prominence as a top professional rider on the premier motorcycle circuits of the world.

He was born in 1927, the son of Harry and Kath Dale. His parents built a bungalow No. 1 Saundergate Lane in front of their haulage business and Dickie went to school in Kirton until the age of 14. He sang in Wyberton Church choir. He started work as a fitter with the Boston Diesel Engine Company before joining the family business three years later. He was drafted into the RAF as a flight mechanic in 1945 and served for three years. He worked on a wide variety of aircraft from Tiger Moths to Meteors. Whilst based at Cranwell he bought his first motorcycle, a 1939 A.J.S. Silver Streak, for transport home at the weekends.

This machine fired his interest in the sport and he began to attend grass track events. In the RAF he remustered as a motorcycle dispatch rider and his obsession with 'bikes' grew further. In 1945 Boston Motor Cycle Club decided to stage a grass track meeting. Dickie enthusiastically entered on a 'grass special' that his near neighbour, Frank Walker, had built just prior to the outbreak of war. Dickie won all his heats, some finals and £12 prize money. His racing career had begun.

Dickie Dale

Dickie Dale no.25

After more grass track meetings he tried his first road circuit in 1946 on a 350cc Norton at Cadwell Park. His success that season caught the eye of Austin Munks, the four times Manx Grand Prix winner and Leverton car dealer. He supplied him with a 500cc Norton and another close friend, Sam Coupland, provided a 350cc Velocette. After his demob from the RAF these two bikes enabled him to get convincing results on the English circuits in 1948. Sam Coupland and Dickie spent much time together. In fact Sam's house stood on the seven mile straight at Frithville and this section of road was used for test runs. The story is that the local bobby was 'in on this' and turned a blind eye, and ear, to such goings-on.

He won his first Isle of Man race in the September on a Guzzi. It was a runaway win, nine and a half minutes ahead of the second man. About this time road haulage businesses were nationalised, and the family firm was sold. Dickie became a professional rider and quickly established himself as the UK's top non-team rider. In 1951 he was signed on by Norton.

A contemporary magazine article said of him: *He faces the future quietly, almost diffidently, for that is his way. Dale appears to be retiring to an exceptional degree and has to be coaxed into conversation and drawn out before he will give an opinion. He is a serious young man who does not smoke, drinks in only extreme moderation and thinks deeply.*

Thus he became team mate to the all conquering and international star, Geoff Duke. Sadly he immediately contracted tuberculosis and spent most of 1951 in a sanatorium in Dorchester. However this long absence from the track did not diminish his skills. After a season with Norton he was recruited first by the Gilera team and then MV. In 1956, just before marrying Australian born Phyllis, he joined the Moto Guzzi team and went to live at Varenna near the factory in Italy for two years. He remained in contact with his friends at home and was President of the Boston Motor Cycle Club for several years.

For the last three years of his career he rode a variety of machines continuing to have successes until 30th April 1961. On that day, while leading the rain-swept 500cc race on Germany's notoriously difficult Nurburgring, Dickie Dale crashed, suffering injuries from which he died while being airlifted to hospital in Bonn. A memorial service was held in St. Leodegar's Church. His ashes were scattered according to his wishes along the seven mile straight and the urn buried under Sam Coupland's lawn.

On Low Road corner 1945. Margaret Garwell, Madge Bontoft, Joan Garwell, Joan Burr.

Army Cadet camp behind Wyberton Park 1946, including Jack Ladds, Cliff Euerby, Derek Falkinder, Don Broughton, 'Tubby' Baker.

Wyberton Airfield by Stuart Lowther

Wyberton Airfield is alongside the Boardsides which is the A1121 road to Sleaford. It consists of two hangars with workshop and refuelling facilities and an unlicensed 600 metre runway. It is currently mainly used by occassional light aircraft and for storage and maintenace work.

It is thought to have first been used as an airfield in 1935. That year the grazing animals were temporarily removed to make way for a display by Sir Alan Cobham's Flying Circus and spectators were invited to take a short flight at a cost of seven shillings and sixpence per trip. At that time the field was owned by Mr. Bailey of 'Bailey and Alexander', the dispensing chemists in Boston.

The Boston Flying Club was formed on October 21st 1949 with one Auster J4 aeroplane and forty founder members. Several were ex-RAF and others pre-war private pilots. Seven enrolled for flying instruction. Richard Hardy was elected President and G.N. Snarey flying instructor. The field was approved by the Ministry of Aviation as a public licensed airfield and a 'blister' hangar erected. This first housed the J4, Ted Moffat's Gemini and a Miles Magister which had recently been restored by Bill Holderness in his nearby garage.

Airfield in 1961 with 2 Austers and a Morris Minor van

Wyberton airfield became well used and caused many vehicles travelling along the Boardsides to reduce their speed and even to stop to view the flying, much to the concern of those less interested in matters aeronautical. The field also became the home of the Boston Aeromodellers' Club who spent many Sunday mornings flying their radio-controlled models whenever the weather proved suitable.

Subsidiary companies were formed for charter flights, light aircraft transport, servicing and maintenance as well as refuelling. There was a regular newspaper collection service from Nottingham to Boston for some time. Skegness airfield was developed in conjunction with Wyberton and became very popular with the Butlin's holiday makers for many years. More than a little interest was aroused when three of the strange looking aircraft which were used during the making of the film *'Those Magnificent Men in their Flying Machines'* landed at the airfield to refuel during 1964, when some scenes were shot near the coast at Skegness.

Clifford Annis, an ex-RAF pilot, was appointed Director and manager of the various enterprises. Several more aircraft were acquired by the company including some Austers, a Tiger Moth and a DeHavilland Rapide.

During the early part of 1949 the Auster Aircraft Company developed crop dusting and spraying equipment for the Auster Autocar at a time when ground spraying was in its infancy. This was to be in great demand in the flat, intensively farmed lands of eastern England. The first aircraft to be fitted with this equipment was delivered to Boston Air Transport in mid-October 1949.

1951 saw the formation of Aerial Spraying Contractors Limited with directors Richard Hardy, Fred Collins and P.C. Andrews, who was the designer and manufacturer of the specialised equipment. With a few modifications the equipment was fitted to three Auster Aiglets and a contract was secured to spray insecticide in what was then the Anglo-Egyptian Sudan. The three aircraft were flown the 3200 miles from Wyberton airfield to Khartoum and on to Wad Medani on the Blue Nile where the Gezira Cotton growing areas had been established after the construction of the Sennar Dam in 1926. This operation proved a great success and the contract was renewed and enlarged for the following four years and the fleet of Aiglets increased to six. Bostonian Wilf Pearson AFC was appointed chief pilot and Leslie Hewitt, from Wyberton,

Director and ground manager for the whole of the operations in the UK and the Sudan. Other Wybertonians on the permanent staff of Aerial Spraying Contractors were Albert Hitch, Mike Ellis, Harold Ellis and Stuart Lowther (the author). Additional freelance pilots were appointed for the annual, three month, overseas contracts and the ground crews were seconded from Hardy and Collins, the local agrochemical suppliers.

The Aiglets would take off from Wyberton airfield early morning in July/August, heavily laden with equipment, tools and spares and additional fuel tanks. However each had the minimum of navigational aids namely, an ex-RAF magnetic compass and chart, a school atlas but no radio facilities of any kind. An adventurous route was taken across the Channel to Le Touquet, over France, following the Mediterranean coast to Sicily and across to Tunis, keeping an eye out for the island of Pantallaria to check the course. The route then continued across North Africa to Cairo and followed the Nile upstream to Khartoum. There were many overnight and refuelling stops as well as forced delays owing to visa difficulties. The contracts were fulfilled and the return journey made during December when weather conditions were not always so favourable.

There were two tragic accidents during this time when, in 1952, one returning aircraft was lost in the Mediterranean. Both the pilot, Joe Teesdale, and his passenger, Ernest Thomas, were killed. Another aircraft crashed during a spraying operation the same year, when Pete Bushby was killed. Aerial Spraying Contractors went into voluntary liquidation in 1956. The contracts were taken over by a new company formed by Cliff Annis, Lincolnshire Aerial Spraying Contractors. They contracted out aircraft and pilots for the work in the UK and the now independent Sudan for several more years.

Boston Aero Club was formed on April 7th (Good Friday) 1950 and a rally of some thirty aircraft took part. The official opening was performed in the afternoon by the Mayor of Boston and visitors had the chance to fly in one of the many aircraft available. Towards the end of the afternoon a tragic accident occurred when an Auster Autocar took off to return to Elstree. It performed a short display, went into a spin but recovered at too low a level and crashed into the bank of the South Forty Foot drain, killing the pilot and his two passengers.

During the 1950's, 60's and 70's the airfield was in full use as a registered airfield for Boston and district offering crop dusting, crop spraying, charter facilities and aircraft servicing and maintenance. At its peak there was a north-south runway as well as the present east-west one. As the agricultural contracts diminished owing to improved ground application methods and an increase in spray drift complaints, the field was reduced in size and the north-south runway was closed. The northern end of the field was then used by the Boston Rugby club who constructed a clubhouse on the eastern edge alongside the Boston Aero Club on Great Fen Road. Commercial development then took place on the southern section of the field which left a very limited east-west runway and a small aircraft parking area. There is currently a proposal to develop the whole site as a leisure/recreational area thereby depriving the district of an amenity which has served the area for the past half century.

Footnote: In the early days of aviation the first airfield in the Boston area was established at Freiston Shore, situated across the Haven from Wyberton Marsh. This airfield was the training field for the Royal Flying Corps during the 1914-1918 conflict. After the war it was abandoned for general flying but used occasionally by the flying circuses which were very popular at that time.

The Phoenix Flyer and a Piper Pawnee 1964

The Royal Mail coach passing the Pincushion Inn 1830 by Glynn Williams

Communications

Roads and Lanes by Richard Austin and Lilian Brabham

Today in Wyberton there are 52 roads and lanes. Some are old established roads that have been in existence for many centuries but about half of them have been built in the last 50 years to service new housing developments. The complete list of roads is included at the end of this book.

Road Maintenance

Until about 1840 almost all the roads in the Parish were mud and grass tracks. The two major exceptions were what are now the London Road and the Swineshead Road, both of which had been Turnpike Roads.

Road maintenance in Wyberton was a great problem as the nearest quarry was at least twenty miles away. Stone only began to be affordable in the mid 19th century. Before a road had a hard surface, when it was wet animal hooves and cart wheels quickly turned it into a boggy quagmire. Most soil in the parish has a high clay content so this difficulty was particularly acute. To reduce the problem, silt (fine sand) was quarried to spread on the lanes and roads to fill in the ruts and to make them higher and drier. At times it was applied to a depth of eighteen inches. One tonne of silt is required to cover a road 10 foot wide to this depth for every yard run. In the Victorian era the cost was 8d. to 10d. per tonne to dig, cart and spread. The silt was obtained by digging pits in those places where it could be found. Most of these pits have been filled in but there is still one on the Great Fen Road at Rectory Farm. There was also a large silt pit on Silt Pit Lane opposite Silt Pit Farm which was filled with household waste in the 1960's. It was the responsibility of the Parish to keep the roads in a reasonable state. In the Church Vestry minutes there are several references to the matter. For example, in 1822 a rood of land (0.25 acres) was purchased by the Parish for *silt for the highways.*

Over the centuries this work was done by the men of the village who were obliged to give four days per year for road mending. In 1563 a law was passed increasing this to six days. In the eighteenth and nineteenth centuries the unemployed of the Village were also engaged for this work under the direction of the Parish Surveyor of the Highways. For the labourers, the Poor Book of 1826 quotes a rate of pay of 18d. per day. Silt continued to be used in farm yards and as flooring in farm buildings as late as the 1960's. When compacted and dry it can be as hard as concrete.

One minor road running between Church Lane and Streetway still remains as a 'silt' lane to this day. Recently named Franks Lane it once would have been a main route to Wyberton Roads.

Stepping stones were also a feature of the roads of Wyberton. They were laid in those parts of a road which were persistently wet and boggy and would have been very important before the days of wellingtons. The village records refer to them along what is now Causeway and also on Church Lane at the junction with Franks Lane.

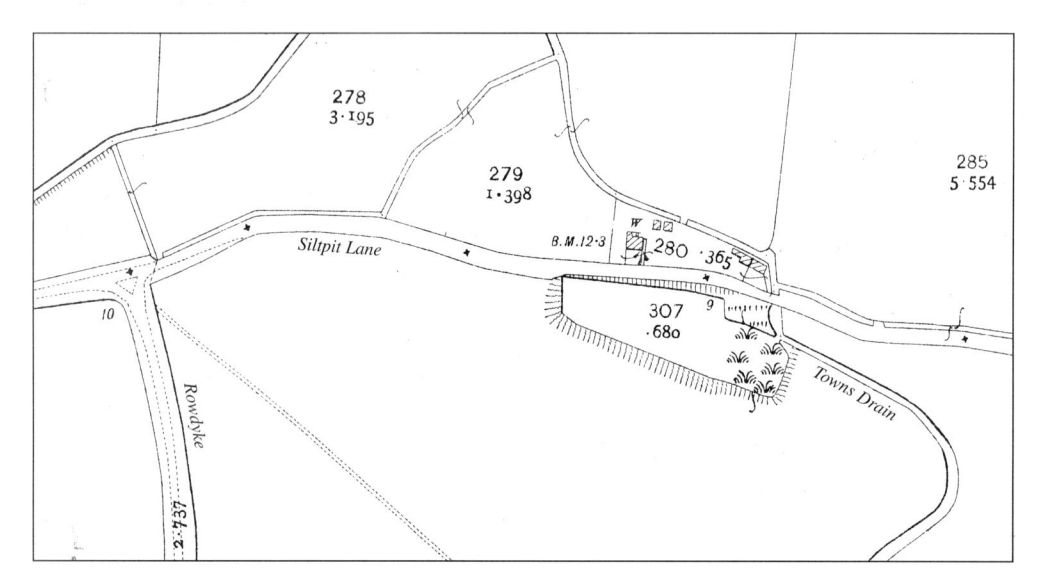

Site of Silt Pit on Siltpit Lane

Silt pit, Silt Pit Lane 1950. Josie Brotherton with her cousin Christine Sharp

In 1837, for the first time, the Select Vestry ordered shingle for surfacing roads. 80 tons were used on Causeway. It was clearly thought to be a big improvement because the following year a further 800 tons of shingle from Wolverton was ordered to improve a one mile stretch of West End Road. It cost 3s.6d. per ton delivered to The Black Sluice. A horse and cart would normally carry one and a half tonnes so this represents a massive haulage job when the boat came in!

From then on there was a rolling programme of applying shingle to the main roads of the village. In about 1870 when W. H. Wheeler was the Borough Engineer he began to surface some of these roads with three inch down granite chippings. By this date the new railway system had sufficiently reduced transport costs. Tar began to be used early in the 19th century on main roads but it was not until the 1930's that tarring became a regular practice on side roads.

Turnpike Roads

In the eighteenth century the need for a better long distance road system which could be used in all weathers became an urgent issue. Before that time most long journeys were made on horseback. For example, in 1554 when Boston Corporation had some business in London it paid Mr. Wilkinson of 'Wiberton' 3s. 3d. for riding there on two occasions. By 1750 the industrial revolution was under way and trade was expanding. Hence the turnpike road system was established by Acts of Parliament.

In 1758 two roads passing through Wyberton were given this new status. They were the route from Boston to Spalding (via Kirton and Sutterton) and Boston to Grantham (via Swineshead and Donington). These were what are now called London Road and Swineshead Road. Trusts were set up with the responsibility of funding, building and keeping up the repairs of this new type of road and they were wider and better constructed than the other roads in the parish. In some parts, to avoid flooding or low lying ground, the roads were built up. This was called 'ramparting', hence the popular name 'Swineshead Ramper'. Turnpike roads were marked with substantial milestones, many of which suvive and are 'listed'. There is one by the bus shelter opposite the Pincushion Inn and another at the end of Wortleys Lane on Swineshead Road.

To pay for the upkeep of the roads, toll houses were established at key points and here travellers paid for the privilege of using the road. Some roads leading on to the turnpike were cut off from it in order that traffic could not use the road without paying. The tolls were at fixed rates of a few pence for carts, flocks of sheep, herds of cattle, flocks of geese and so on and there were special concessions for people going to market and fixed rates for those who wished to pay for the equivalent of a 'season ticket'.

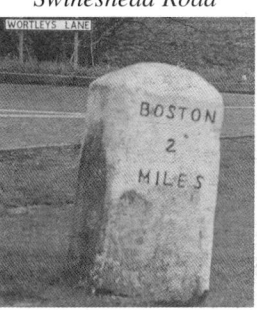

The tolls on the road collected at the Black Sluice amounted to as much as £2465 a year, a sum in excess of those collected by the toll gates leading into Lincoln.

Milestones opposite the Pincushion and on Swineshead Road

Stage coaches which used these roads did not need to stop at the toll gates but, having warned the keeper that they were coming by a bleat on the horn, were allowed through as the gates were hurriedly opened. Scheduled services were run to London and other towns. The last London coach ran on 16th October 1847, the day before the first passenger train ran on the newly opened line.

The actual construction of the roads posed some problems. They were made twelve feet wide and had a core of gravel, stone and silt. Gravel and shingle were brought in by sea through Boston or Fosdyke and cost about four shillings and sixpence a ton. Gravel was also brought over land from the Horncastle area at a cost of five to six shillings a ton. Seven tons of gravel was needed to construct a road 12 ft wide for a distance of 1 chain. The same amount of gravel would repair 1½ chains of a road which had already been 'metalled'.

The days of the turnpike roads were limited. The coming of the railways resulted in a rapid decline in the traffic on the roads and the toll system was abolished. The present main roads in the parish, the A52 to Grantham and the former A16 following what became known as London Road, are main roads today although the route of the railway line, which had killed the turnpike system, is now the main road between Boston and Spalding.

In 1892 the upkeep of the roads was passed from the Trusts established to set up the roads to the council, indeed to Holland County Council, which continued to be responsible until Holland became part of the whole county of Lincolnshire in the 1970's.

Silt pit at Rectory Farm, Wyberton Fen

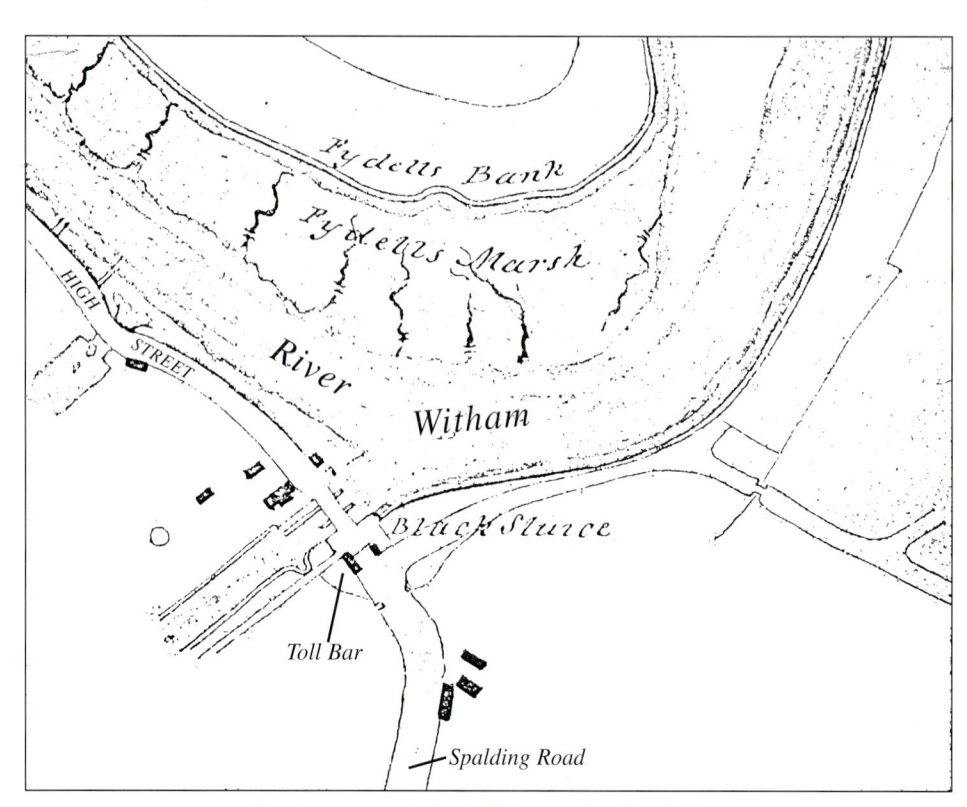

The Location of the Toll Bar at the Black Sluice

London Road in 1986

First Telephones

Did you know that the first telephones in Wyberton were installed in 1908? In that year the National Telephone Company installed three miles of wires along *Low Road and District* and William Dennis and Sons then installed a further one mile of wires to their Streetway property.

Fuel by Richard Austin

Gas and electricity are the main sources of domestic fuel today, together with coal and wood to a lesser extent.

Gas came to the village in the 1930's, first being available along London Road and then gradually being extended to the other roads. This was what we now call *Town Gas*. Conversion to North Sea Gas was in 1973. Electricity was first supplied by the Boston Electrical Supply Company (BESCO) in about 1930 but it was the 1950's before the outlying parts of the parish were able to 'switch on'.

In earlier centuries coal, wood, cow dung and peat have all been used in great quantities.

The earliest detailed records date from 1530 at which time wood was a prominent item in almost every probate inventory. This indicates that trees were a greater feature of the parish landscape than they are today. Elm was very common but this magnificent species sadly was entirely killed off by Dutch Elm Disease in the 1970's. Willow, too, was widespread in the past. Peat, which was commonly called 'turves', is also mentioned in the 1500's as a fuel. At that time there were still beds of peat about 15 miles to the north and west in the fresh water fens.

Another major fuel source was dried cow dung, as it still is in third world countries today. It was fashioned into balls and dried. These were called 'dythes'. A lady who rode side-saddle through the district in about 1700 describes, with distaste, offensive piles of dythes being stacked against the walls of each house. The last reference to them in Wyberton occurs in 1714, in the inventory of Henry Dickinson.

Coal has also been a major fuel source for a long time. It is first mentioned in 1582, amongst the belongings of Richard Smyth. At this time coal would have been shipped down the east coast from the mines of Northumberland. It continued to be brought into Boston by ship and barge until the opening of the railway.

Vernon Higham on his BESCO bike 1945

Wyberton's two Railways by Stephen Peel

One hundred and fifty years ago the railways revolutionized life in Wyberton by allowing cheap mass-produced goods to be brought in. The village began to export perishable foods, creating a new industry which still employs many local people. Either Kirton or Boston stations were used.

The advantages to Wyberton probably escaped the notice of the leading citizens of Boston who sought a railway line to Nottingham during the 1840's. These merchants hoped that the railway would bring coal and other goods to be exported through Boston docks. However, railways were expensive to build and Boston was unable to support such a line by itself. The alternative was to use Boston as a through station on a line between two big cities. In 1845 such a line was proposed between London and York with a loop line from Peterborough to Doncaster, via Boston. Since it was the only proposal that was likely to be built, Boston council supported this scheme. In 1846 Parliament passed plans to build both this line and a line to Ambergate in Derbyshire. The Great Northern Railway Company began to build towards Boston in 1847. The line was opened on October 17th 1848. The first train left Peterborough at 6 a.m. and passed through Wyberton around 7.30 a.m. A holiday was proclaimed and official functions and private parties were held all day.

Meanwhile, financial support was not found to continue the Boston to Ambergate line beyond the east side of Grantham. Consequently the "Boston and Midland Railway and Docks Company" was formed in 1852. This company intended to build the railway and improve Boston docks. A clause in the Act of Parliament (needed to build the railway) required the company to erect an eight foot high fence between the railway and Boardsides road. Because of lack of money, the line took seven years to build and was finally opened on April 12th 1859. A special train left Grantham at 12.30 p.m. and passed through Wyberton shortly before 2 p.m. The company never made a profit and the line was taken over by the Great Northern Railway in 1865 in order to prevent a rival company from buying it.

Over the next 100 years the changes that occurred were caused by national, rather than local needs. On January 1st 1923 rationalisation of the railways took place and over 100 smaller railway companies were merged to form four large railway companies, Boston becoming part of the London and North Eastern Railway. By this time the heyday of the railways was passing, roads had improved and transport such as buses and lorries was more flexible, reliable and quicker.

The railway system was nationalised in 1947 and increased road competition during the 1950's forced British Railways to concentrate on the more profitable main lines. Demand for branch lines fell until they became too expensive to keep. Consequently the line between Lincoln and Peterborough via Wyberton and Boston was closed on October 5th 1970. Strangely, Council grants and holiday traffic have enabled Wyberton's other line to Grantham to remain open. Perhaps the citizens of Boston in 1840 were right after all!

A 'Little Sharpie' engine in Grantham station c.1850; the type of engine used when the Boston lines were opened.

An 0-6-0 loco near Calders

The morning express to London in the 1950's

Wyberton High Bridge signal box, demolished in 1984

Last train on the line passing the Tytton Lane East crossing keeper's house in 1971

Wyberton and Frampton Home Guard, Wyberton Parish Hall 1943

Wars

The Civil War by Richard Austin

On Wednesday the 3rd and Thursday the 4th of October 1643, a 5,000 strong Parliamentary Army with artillery, camp followers and baggage carts streamed through Wyberton along what is now London Road. This was some thirteen months after the outbreak of the Civil War between King Charles I and Parliament. This section of the 'Roundhead' army was known as the Eastern Association and was commanded by the Earl of Manchester. Colonel Oliver Cromwell was in charge of cavalry. The Army had just captured and secured Kings Lynn and had marched via Spalding to Boston to prepare for their next encounter with the Royalists. Boston and Wyberton had strong leanings to the Parliamentary cause and the troops were made welcome. They were to have a weekend 'break' in the town before they pushed north to lay siege to Bolingbroke Castle and on to clinch a decisive victory at Winceby on Wednesday. About 500 Royalists and Roundheads were killed in this Battle.

There can be no doubt that the village became involved in supplying men as well as provisions and forage and probably horses to the army at this dramatic time. Later Cromwell and some of the army returned to spend the winter in Boston.

At least one resident of Wyberton had other affiliations; that was the Rector, Canon Hugh Barcroft DD. He was an unswerving supporter of the Stuart side. In 1644 he was brought before the Earl of Manchester and on the evidence of 16 of his parishioners, was deprived of his living. However, with the crowning of King Charles II, he was reinstated and with some satisfaction wrote in the Church Register - *Christenings after ye 25th of December 1660 that being the day that Dr. Barcroft reentered into his parsonage of Wiberton.*

In 1649 there is a record of a Wyberton parishioner, George Croft, serving with Cromwell's Army in Ireland.

World War One - 1914 to 1918 by Richard Austin

The Wortleys in 1919. Standing: Joe, Fred, George, Jack. Seated: Elizabeth, Will, Benjamin.

The First World War affected many aspects of village life. At the outbreak of hostilities a prominent personality was Captain Meaburn Staniland whose family home was Wyberton House on Streetway. He was Town Clerk but also commanded the Boston Volunteer Territorial Unit which was C company of the 4th Lincoln's. He was killed in France in 1915. Captain Staniland had four young sons and sadly his widow died some six months later.

It was a time of patriotic fervour and many young men were encouraged to volunteer for military service by peer pressure. Amongst them were all five sons of Benjamin and Elizabeth Wortley. Amazingly they all survived the war although William was badly gassed. Benjamin Wortley was a farmer who lived at Highfield House, next to the mill house on West End Road.

Fred North

Fred North is an example of a Wyberton lad who enlisted in 1914. He was the son of John and Harriet North who lived in the Gate House at the Tytton Lane Railway Crossing. John was a plate layer with the Great Northern Railway Company and Harriet's job was to open the crossing gates. Young Fred attended Wyberton School until the age of 13 and on leaving in 1910 went to work for W. Dennis & Sons. He enlisted into the Royal Engineers at the outbreak of war as a Driver and saw service in France and Belgium. His decorations included the 1914 - 1915 Star Medal, the British War Medal and the Victory Medal. The British War Medal indicates he was involved in some of the most terrible battles of that war.

Unfortunately Fred was gassed and spent some time recuperating in Frampton Hall. The Dennis family had transformed part of their home there into a sanatorium for wounded soldiers.

Fred married Florence who was a cook at the Hall and in due time began work as a horseman back on the farm. They lived at Algarkirk and raised four children although he suffered poor health following his traumatic experiences in France. He died in 1936 aged 40 and was buried in Algarkirk Churchyard with full military honours.

Fred North 1914

A class L23 Zeppelin

Zeppelin bombs Wyberton

On the night of Saturday, 2nd September 1916 Emily Emerson, aged ten, was asleep at Slate House Farm on the Boardsides when she was rudely wakened by a loud explosion. The house windows were shattered and ceilings came down. Her mother appeared through the dust to check that she was not injured and announced that she thought they had been bombed by a 'Zep'. Indeed they had!

The 110lb high explosive bomb dropped by hand from Zeppelin L23 landed right on the Wyberton boundary, in the dyke to the west of the brick and slate farmhouse. Several chickens were killed but there were no other casualties. Emily was told by her parents that the bomb had been aimed at a train which had been passing at the time. For several days the crater became a sightseeing venue for the locals.

The 'Q' class Zeppelin was one of 16 dirigibles that had been sent that night from near Bremerhaven in North Germany to cause mayhem and destruction in Eastern England with a load of 1500 kg of high explosive and incendiary bombs. The L23 was 585 feet long and 61 feet in diameter, that is about the length of two football pitches and the width of a cricket wicket. It flew in over the Wash powered by its four noisy 240 hp Maybach engines. It came in over Wyberton dropping the bomb at Slate House Farm and then made a wide loop which took it near Gosberton and back to Boston. Here it dropped six more bombs which killed one person and severely injured another. The Zeppelin,

117

with a crew of 17, then turned south passing near Holbeach and Gorefield before returning north to release another bomb near Springfields at Spalding. It then headed for home out across the Wash.

The commander, Kapitanleutant Wilhelm Ganzel, filed in his log when he landed at the Nordholz base at 8.05 am that he had bombed Norwich! It had taken him 18 hours to fly the 805 miles at an average speed of 45mph using 4000 litres of fuel.

The L23 was shot down in flames off Jutland on 21st August 1917 by a Sopwith Camel fighter using incendiary bullets. None of the crew survived.

Fatalities of World War I

Wyberton had a 'lucky' war and suffered many fewer casualties in proportion to its population than any other village in the area. Indeed Wyberton is the only local parish without a war memorial.

A 110 lb Zeppelin bomb

Martin Middlebrook in his book *Boston at War* projected that Wyberton could have expected about 16 of its young men to have been killed using average casualty data. In fact only five are known:-

Captain Meaburn Staniland (Boston Territorials) of Wyberton House, Streetway, was killed by a stray bullet while inspecting men at their posts on the Ypres Salient on 29th July 1915. He is commemorated on a plaque on the wall inside Wyberton Church.

Lance Corporal Fred Dawson (West Yorkshire Regiment) was killed in action on 28th September 1916 on the Somme and is commemorated on the St. Thomas' Church Memorial.

Rifleman Arthur Bourne (Kings Royal Rifle Corps) was killed in action at Passchendaele on 20th September 1917 and is also listed on the War Memorial at St. Thomas' Church.

Gunner George Henry Heppenstall (Royal Field Artillery) died on 15th November 1918 and is buried in Boston Cemetery, Section G, Grave 321 and is commemorated on the Boston War Memorial.

Frederick Brown - Deck hand on the Steam Trawler 'Lindsey' drowned when his boat was sunk by a mine whilst fishing on 10th September 1920. His name is included on the Tower Hill Memorial, London, to the Missing of the Merchant Navy.

The Second World War -1939 to 1945 by Richard Austin

War was declared at eleven o'clock on Sunday 3rd September, 1939 and was announced to the nation in a radio broadcast by Prime Minister Chamberlain. At the time Vernon Higham was a member of the church choir and recalled that there was the usual large congregation that morning. After the broadcast someone rushed into the Church with the news and handed a note to the Verger who in turn passed it on to the Rector, the Reverend William Ford. He interrupted the Morning Service to read out the announcement and said some special prayers. The war was to affect every aspect of life in the village for many years.

The first thing to happen was the arrival in Boston, that very day, of bus loads of refugees from Hull. These were dispersed to every village and families allocated to households which had any spare room. For example, Jim and Lucy Garwell of Church View on the Low Road were asked to have a mother with two small children. However they did not stay more than a few weeks as Hull was not bombed at this stage of the war.

Identity cards were issued. Men not in essential jobs signed up or were conscripted into the armed forces. The remainder, almost without exception, volunteered for other duties. These included the Home Guard, air raid wardens, firemen, special constables or the rescue services. Women too were involved. Some joined the Forces or the Women's Land Army, others found themselves doing the work formerly done by the conscripted men. The Rectory was used as a hostel for the Women's Land Army. For the first time it became both respectable and patriotic for married women to work. Ladies also joined the Red Cross and the Women's Voluntary Service. Jam making, pigs in the back garden and growing potatoes on every spare piece of land, including the lawn, was greatly encouraged. Everyone was bombarded with ideas on how to make meagre supplies stretch further. There was even propaganda to bath in no more than six inches of water. Petrol, coal and clothing were strictly rationed by a system of coupons. Most items of food were rationed but not potatoes and bread although the latter was rationed for a brief period in 1947. As with the First World War, prisoners of war worked on local farms.

The Sherwood Foresters and Queen's Regiments were billeted in the district as a precaution against invasion. The Leicesters were involved in setting up and manning an aircraft searchlight on London Road near the Village Hall. Jim Sharp, the local blacksmith was called in to help them. They also established a searchlight and ack-ack anti-aircraft gun battery at Cut End, the foundations of which can be found today. Cecil Brotherton remembers lending his horses to carry ammunition, spares and fuel along the river bank to the site. Two pill boxes were built at Wyberton Roads and two more at Cut End.

John Cheer 1939

During the first two years of the war plenty of enemy aircraft were seen and heard over the parish, mainly on their way to bomb airfields to the north and industrial towns such as Sheffield and Derby. No bombs were dropped in Wyberton although Frampton and Skirbeck were not so lucky. Later it was more common to hear the drone of heavily laden allied aircraft on their way to bomb Germany.

Church Choir 1939. Back row: L. Foster, C. Matson, B. Simmons, F. Blake, H. Seaser. 2nd row: R. Gill, Mr. Kirby, C. Goodley, F. Burton, Mr. Chase, Mr. Blake, R. Staples. 3rd row: V. Higham, J. Richmond, A. Goodley, G. Horry, Rev Ford, B. Adcock, L. Hewitt, L. Heppenstall, W Featherstone. Front row: ?, R. Clarke, M. Matson, P. Seaser, J. Gill, E. Richmond, W. Matson.

Auxiliaries

In 1940 John Cheer was approached to join a new organisation which would be very important in the event of a German invasion. He was told that he could not have more information unless he volunteered and signed the Official Secrets Act. Having done this he was then informed that he had joined the regular army and was now a member of the newly formed, top secret Auxiliaries.

The Auxiliaries were the early forerunners of the SAS. Their duty in 1940 was to go underground during an invasion and fight a guerrilla war behind enemy lines. Their life expectancy would be no more than three weeks! In eastern and southern England some 4000 were recruited. They were formed into patrols of up to seven men, each with a sergeant as leader. It was important that every man had an intimate knowledge of his area and many farmers were recruited. Their cover was 202 Battalion of the Home Guard.

Each man was trained in unarmed combat and issued with a revolver. They were also given the very latest high explosives and booby traps to create mayhem behind enemy lines. Patrols practised hard under the direction of training officers Captain Donald Hamilton Hill and Second Lieutenant Eric Dring*. It is thought that they would have given a good account of themselves if they had been put to the test.

Each patrol had one or more well disguised underground hideouts, otherwise known as Operational Bases, which were equipped with bunks for sleeping, lamps, an oil heater and a toilet. The local one was 500 yards north of the Chain Bridge railway crossing. It was built in 1941 using waterproof rock asphalt by contractors John Sheffield and Company at map reference 304440. The area at that time was farmed as small grass fields with high hedges. Today it is one big arable field with no trace of the hideout which was destroyed after the war. This Operational Base was the 'country retreat' for the Boston Patrol which already had two other bases in town, one near the Docks and a second in West Street on a bomb site opposite the Regal Cinema. John Cheer was a member of the Holbeach Patrol and acted as a motor cycle courier for Group Leader Bill Greenwood. John remembered visiting several other patrols. There were bases at Boston, Butterwick, Struggs Hill, Swineshead, Crowland and Sutton Bridge. For security reasons auxiliaries were given no details about other units but, as a courier, John had access to more information of other patrols. He remembered the night that the Invasion was thought to have started when the codeword 'Cromwell' was issued to all units. This meant that conditions were suitable for an invasion. Unfortunately it was misinterpreted and several people were killed by overzealous troops but none locally, although a bridge over the Hobhole drain was blown up.

The Swineshead hideout still exists and is in good repair on The Manwarings. It is well worth a visit....if you can find it!

* Eric Dring returned to the family farm at Holland Fen after the war and became a very successful farmer.

Home Guard

On the 14th May 1940 the Minister for War, Anthony Eden, announced the formation of the Local Volunteer Defence Force. Winston Churchill later decreed that the name be changed to the Home Guard. By the end of June one and a half million men had been recruited.

The Wyberton contingent met and trained at the Parish Hall. In the early days there were no rifles or uniform; they had to drill with broomstick handles. When the first Browning Automatic 303 rifle was issued it was allocated to Harry Hill, being the best sharp shooter in the squad. His orders on the day of the invasion were to ring the bells of St. Leodegar's Church and then be a sniper from the Church tower. In time uniforms and rifles were allocated to the squad so that by 1943, when the photograph was taken, they were a force to be reckoned with.

Auxiliary hide-out at the Manwarings, Swineshead with Cecil Thornalley and Eddie Welberry

In the early days of the war there was paranoia about German spies. The Home Guard therefore set up road blocks at which everyone was ordered to show their identity cards. If anyone failed to stop the orders were to fire two warning shots and then one to kill. This resulted in tragic accidents elsewhere in the country but fortunately none in Wyberton. The volunteers all had full time work but were required to put in many hours of duty at night and in their spare time.

Fatalities of World War 2

Sergeant Clifford Hopkinson was a Wireless/Airgunner with 44 Squadron Flying Lancasters. His aircraft crashed near the target on a bombing raid to Munich on 2nd October 1941. There were no survivors and seven other aircraft were lost on this mission.

Private George Henry Lyon served with the 6th Battalion of the Lincolnshire Regiment. He was killed in a German ambush of a North African village in 1943 and is buried at Tabarka Ras Rajel in Tunisia.

Private William Henry Nixon of the 1st/6th South Staffordshire Regiment died on 6th August, 1944 two months after the 'D' Day landings. He is buried at Calvados in Northern France.

Corporal James Robert Norris of the 6th Battalion of the Lincolnshire Regiment died of malaria in 1943 in Italy and is buried in the Caserta War Cemetery.

Lance Corporal Thomas William Wright of the 10th Company Royal Pioneer Corps. was severely wounded during the landing at Bayeaux and died in hospital on 1st August, 1944.

Pilot Officer Colin H. Curtis No. 101 Squadron died in 1942.

Aircraftman Harold J. Nix No. 84 Squadron died in 1942.

William Clarke - no details available.

All the above names appear on a plaque inside Wyberton Church.

Brigadier General Aldecron c.1916

Headstone in Wyberton Churchyard

Brigadier General R. L. Aldecron by Richard Austin

For his last 13 years Brigadier General Aldecron lived at Wyberton Park with his daughter and son-in-law Mr. and Mrs. Blackie. He was buried in 1966 near the church door at the end of a very colourful and eventful life.

As a young officer he saw service in the Anglo - Egyptian Sudan in 1896 and fought at the Battles of Obduman and Atbara. He also served in South Africa as a mounted infantry officer in the Boer War and was severely wounded. In the First World War he commanded the 148th and the 124th Infantry Brigades which fought in the Battle of the Somme in 1916 and the Battle of Passchendaele in 1917. He is believed to have been the last Brigadier General in the British Army.

Brigadier General Aldecron retired from active army service in 1920 and lived at Culverthorpe Hall near Sleaford and became heavily involved in public work. He was for many years County Commissioner of the Boy Scouts and organised local football teams which formed the nucleus of the present day leagues. He was a County Councilor, a Deputy Lieutenant and a Justice of the Peace. He was a keen sportsman, a skier and hunted with the Belvoir hounds. In the World War 2 he commanded the East Kesteven Battalion of the Home Guard.

Garden Party, Wyberton Rectory 1937

Boston Wheelers at the start of their 25 mile road race to Pinchbeck and back c.1948 outside the Pincushion

Wyberton
Past and Present

Memories by Lilian Brabham and Alison Austin

Many memories have been stirred by the search for information for this History of Wyberton. For example, in the 1930's several tradesmen made doorstep deliveries to houses in Wyberton.

Mr. Whittaker had a brown van and every Friday delivered groceries and candles as well as paraffin for the oil lamps which people used in their houses. Mr. Barrand, the baker brought round fresh bread and cakes from his shop in Mitre Lane every Tuesday, Thursday and Saturday. Mr. Mould was another baker who delivered bread and cakes all over Wyberton in his van. His shop was in High Street.

A special treat on Saturday afternoons was when Jimmy Forman used his motorbike and sidecar to go round the streets selling ice-cream. Then there was Mr. Lambert, who had a shop in Red Lion Street. He visited his customers with a large case containing clothes and linen for sale. A farmer, Mr. Turner was also a butcher and delivered meat.

Some of the things that children used to get up to come to mind. They played games like whip and top and hopscotch or bowling a hoop and skipping. Then you could always go fishing for tiddlers or looking for violets and snowdrops in Rabbit Lane. Eve Warburton remembers playing in the fields after harvest and making tents out of the sacks. Several people recall cycling down to the marshes, playing in the creeks and going home covered in mud. Some of them used to take a tent and camp there.

Children had to run errands, too, like fetching milk in a can from a farmhouse on Streetway. Ruby Hewson was one of many who had to take the accumulator for the wireless all the way to Kirton to be charged up. There was no electricity let alone any television. One farmer would take his lorry into Boston and fetch 20 children from Carlton Road School with their headteacher, Mr. Pearson to help with potato picking. After corn harvest all the children would go gleaning in the fields so that none of the crop was wasted.

When Mr. King was the sexton he used to ring the church bells. They would ring out his name, Old Tom King! In the Church the organ had to be pumped using a long wooden handle (which is still there at the side of the organ). This went on until an electric pump was installed in the late 1940's. Mrs Keal used to play the organ and Denis Heppenstall usually had to do the pumping. There was an old lady called Charlotte Bellamy who rarely left her cottage on Ralphs Lane except on Sundays, when she walked to Church for both the morning and evening services.

Buried in the Churchyard in 1953 was Daniel Stephenson, a railway worker. He was born at Wyberton Roads in 1850. Only a few people will remember him but everyone will have heard of his granddaughter, the former Prime Minister, Margaret Thatcher.

Several people remember a man called Bill Crawley who used to live in a hole in the river bank. Every Friday he walked out from Boston with a pack on his back and spent the weekend in his dugout near the end of Commissioners Road. Inside it was lined and there was a bunk and a stove. He would climb in through a trapdoor in the top of the bank. He kept his food in another hole which was disguised with seaweed.

There was a rifle range by the river at Slippery Gowt. It was used by the army and the territorials for training during the two World Wars and also by the Home Guard. The butts were near the sluice and the firing took place from further up-river. It was closed down for safety reasons after WW2.

Mr. Mould's bread van c.1920

The Old Post Office by the Churchyard c. 1930

Shops

Several Wyberton residents recall shops that have now disappeared. Often they were in the front room of a house sometimes even in a hut.

Wyberton has had several Post Offices. The first was in Mr. King's house by the Church and was there from the end of the last century until the 1920's. The next Post Office was on the Low Road near the Old School and was run by Mr. and Mrs Dillamore in a room in their cottage. Mrs Phyllis Hill remembers that they used to dote on a very large old cat. In the late 1930's Mrs Simmonds took over and ran a Post Office in the kitchen of her bungalow, also on the Low Road, for about ten years until they moved away. This then left Wyberton without a Post Office for several years until one opened on Granville Avenue.

There were other shops, too. Reg and Eve Clarke recall that in 1935 Mrs Casburn had a general store at no. 2 Granville Avenue. Then Joshua and Jessie Clark had a cafe in a wooden building on London Road, opposite the Bramley Gardens Farmhouse. They served refreshments from about 1936 until the war in 1939. You could get tea and buns and pop. For several years there was a fish and chip shop in a hut in the Pincushion yard. This was there until 1952 when it moved to Saundergate Lane. As recently as the late 1960's Mrs Barker had a little general store in the front room of her bungalow at 94 Tytton Lane West.

Shopping in 1999

Shops in Wyberton are situated in two areas. In the Parthian Avenue vicinity are the smaller shops dating from the 1950's that serve the immediate local community. At the west end of the parish are the new large out-of-town retail establishments that attract customers from Boston and the surrounding district.

The Post Office/General Store run by Bob Cory and his family is situated on Granville Avenue. At the centre of the Parthian Avenue estate there are three shops. The *Spar* Shop run by the Paddison family is a General Store that now includes the newsagents. Next to this is the *Jolly Fryer*, a fish and chip shop, and the third premises is currently a video library. On Saundergate Lane is *In Style*, a hairdressing salon.

At the other end of the parish by the Chain Bridge is *Oldrid's Downtown* furniture store. The last decade has also brought the large *Tesco* Supermarket and on the opposite side of the Swineshead Road, *Old MacDonald's Farm Produce*. Wyberton's most recent arrival is B&Q, with their DIY Superstore on the Westbridge site.

Parthian Avenue shops, early 1950's

Wyberton's Industries

Calders and Grandidge

Calders and Grandidge is the largest manufacturing business in the parish. The site now includes the original business of making and supplying creosoted overhead line wood poles, fencing posts and rails under the name of Calders and Grandidge. The associated housebuilding component manufacturing business on the same site trades under the name of Guildway.

Calders had its origins in Scotland in 1820. The company first came to Boston in 1896 when it opened a sleeper mill on the Dock. Their 36 acre Wyberton site was first acquired in 1930 to supply poles for the rapidly expanding rural electricity and telephone business. It lay between London Road and the LNER railway line with good access to both. The new pole business

Pole yard, Calders and Grandidge

prospered and Calders rapidly became the largest UK supplier. The poles are mainly produced from Scandinavian Scots Pine. They arrive in Wyberton having been shipped into the UK direct from the forest, just stripped of their bark and branches. They are 'seasoned' or dried for six to twelve months in the yard before being pressure treated with creosote or tanolith. Currently the yard produces some 70,000 poles each year.

Since 1945 there has also been a secondary saw milling and manufacturing business. Products have included wooden boxes for the drinks trade, components for cooling towers and finally, today, sections for house building and complete timber-frame houses. In the 1950's many women were employed for making the boxes.

Box making at Calders c.1950

J. Mastenbroek & Co

J Mastenbroek & Co Ltd

In 1971, John Mastenbroek and his family moved to 83 Swineshead Road, Wyberton Fen, bringing with them their newly-formed company. Over the years J Mastenbroek & Co Ltd has grown to become one of the world's leading manufacturers of trenching equipment. Initially specialising in land drainage machinery, the company was forced to diversify in the 1980's when the abolition of farming subsidies decimated the drainage industry. The company now supplies its specialised self-propelled, tracked trenching machinery to projects all around the world where they are used to install all types of pipes and cables for agricultural, civil engineering and utilities applications, both on land and sub-sea.

Red Rose International Limited

Red Rose was founded by Colin Massey in 1990 and the factory on Slippery Gowt Lane built in 1993. The company import and pack fruit from all corners of the globe but particularly all varieties of melons. Their speciality is the yellow honeydew type. Red Rose is arguably the largest trader of melons in the world. Other specialities are mangos and Spanish citrus fruit.

Much of the fruit comes from Europe but in recent years the company has been initiating growing programmes in such countries as Honduras, Costa Rica and Brazil. Red Rose serves most of the major supermarkets. It is 50% owned by Colin Massey and 50% by the Spanish company Jose Canovas Pardo S.L.

Red Rose

Wyberton Clubs and Societies

Some of the clubs and societies meeting in Wyberton are listed below. They serve members of the surrounding parishes as well as the village itself. Some have their own premises but others use a variety of venues.

Scouts

The Scout Association includes Scouts, Cub Scouts and Beavers (for the younger age group). In Wyberton they all come under the umbrella of the 8th Boston (Wyberton) Scout Group. There is currently a combined membership of 75 boys with 7 leaders. Meetings are held in the Scout/W.I. Hut on Tytton Lane East.

The 8th Boston (Wyberton) Boy Scouts and the Wolf Cub Pack were formed in February 1948. The first boys to be enrolled into the Cubs were Terence Brown, Peter Clarke and Richard Crofts. The leaders at that time were B.E. Hird and M.G. Everett.

Guides

In the Guide Association there are Guides, Brownie Guides and Rainbows. For older girls there are Rangers and Young Leaders but these two units are based in Boston. The 1st Wyberton Guides were formed in June 1967, being founded by Pat Hedgecock with assistant Christine Goor and 8 Guides. Their first meeting place was the Old School on the Low Road.

There are 14 Guides at the time of writing and meetings are now held in Wyberton Primary School on Saundergate Lane. Since 1973 four girls have gained their Queen's Guide award and a further seven have received the Baden-Powell Trefoil.

The 1st Wyberton Brownies were also formed in June 1967, meeting at the Old School under the leadership of Mrs Lee and Mrs Bolton. Currently there are 26 Brownies with 3 Guiders, 3 Young Leaders and one Unit Helper and meetings are at the Wyberton School. Because of the large number of children waiting to join the unit, the 2nd Wyberton Brownies was opened in 1997 but they meet at St. Michael's Church Hall, Frampton West. Wyberton Rainbows were formed in 1988.

Women's Institutes

There are two Women's Institutes in Wyberton. The older of the two is the Wyberton Women's Institute which started in 1932. Its founder members included Mrs Benton, Mrs Crabtree and Mrs Cannon. Meetings have always been held in the Wyberton Parish Hall and currently there are 18 members. In the 1930's the group had an active drama section that gave several performances in Boston.

The Wyberton Church End W.I. was formed in 1940 and now meets in the combined Scout/W.I. hut on Tytton Lane East. Founder members included Mrs Pogson, Mrs Sumner, Mrs Cannon, Mrs Hill, Mrs Wilkinson and Mrs Aubin and early meetings were in members' homes. After this a small

8th Boston (Wyberton) Cubs and Scouts 1949

Wyberton Cubs c.1966

corrugated hut on the present site prior to the building of the new hall was used. The site was donated by Mr. J.H. Dell. There are currently 36 members.

Wyberton Theatrical Society

Although this Society still carries the Wyberton name it is no longer a village organisation. From 1947 right through the 1950's it was an active group meeting regularly in the Wyberton Parish Hall where it staged numerous play readings and dramatic productions. The group then moved its base to Boston where it continues as a flourishing amateur society.

Wyberton Over 60's Club

This club was founded in 1984 by Mrs M. Scrupps and the late Mrs E. Fletcher with meetings in the Old Parish Hall. It moved to its current home at the Wyberton Sports and Social Club on the Playing Fields at Causeway so that fewer members had to cross the London Road. There are 74 members and a Christmas party is held every year as well as coach trips, meals out and other activities.

The Happy Time Club

Formed in 1972 with members from Frampton, Kirton and Wyberton, meetings were held first at Kirton Secondary School and latterly in the Wyberton Parish Hall. Although there were 24 members this club unfortunately closed on 31st December 1998 due to lack of numbers.

Football

Wyberton Rangers football team was set up in 1948 by Mr. Alf Fox and Mr. Fred Tunstall who had played international football and at one time was manager and trainer at Boston. The team was sponsored by Notts County through one of its directors, Mr. Linnell who was a friend of Alf Fox. The photograph was taken on the occasion of the Burrell Cup final in which Wyberton Rangers beat Swineshead. One player who gained honours was goalkeeper, Mick Pinner. He played amateur international and Olympic football, and also played occasionally for Manchester, Arsenal and Pegasus.

WI outing to Wedgwood 1965

Wyberton Rangers 1950's. Back row: Mr. Burrell Snr., Robin Everitt, Norman Osgarby, Billy Baxter (Notts County), Maurice Elding, Brian Sharp, Stan Lawrence, Mick Pinner, Eric Houghton, Tommy Lawton (England International), Mr. Burrell.
Front row: John Fox, Ray Smith, Pete Loveley, Gordon Upsall, Sid Williams.

A village football team for Wyberton was started in 1963 initially playing friendly matches but then joining the Boston and District leagues. Before Wyberton had its own playing field, Graves Park at Kirton was used but in 1965 the land for the existing field was purchased. The tea bar from the bank at Frampton Marsh was fetched by Fosdyke Cricket Club and transported by George Hall's horse and cart to Wyberton where it became the dressing room. It is still in use as a store at the Club.

It is difficult to single out any one individual as being the club's founder, but over a long period of time Wyberton Football Club owed much to the services of members Ken Jackson, Ian Smith and Cyril Borrill. During its 30 year history the Inter Wyberton Club has had considerable success, winning both the Saturday and Sunday leagues on several occasions. The Club was accepted into the Lincolnshire League in 1991 and the proudest achievement was in 1995 when Wyberton was the first team from the Boston area to win this league.

Youth football was started in 1964 and soon Wyberton Colts was formed under the direction of Ray Harris. Like the senior team, the Colts have won County, league and cup competitions on numerous occasions. It is one of the most respected clubs in Lincolnshire and attracts youngsters from a 30-mile radius of Wyberton. There are 4 or 5 teams covering the different age groups and about 60 boys involved in any season. This team has been the breeding ground for talented local youngsters and to date six lads have gone on to play for professional teams and some have gained national honours.

In the early 1970s' Mick Vinter played for Notts County and Wrexham and Ian Nimmo for Sheffield Wednesday and Doncaster. They were both Wyberton boys. Other successes came from the surrounding district. In the late 1970's Chris Woods represented England and played in goal for Nottingham Forest and Glasgow Rangers and at the same time Simon Garner played for Blackburn Rovers.

At the present time Julian Joachim plays for Aston Villa and has represented England at U21. Danny Butterfield has joined Grimsby and has been capped for England at U18.

Wyberton has an outstanding record both at adult and junior levels for a village football club.

Wyberton Sports and Social Club

The Wyberton Playing Field Association was formed in 1964 for the purchase of the land on Causeway that was to become the village playing field. This was partly financed by an additional 1d. on the local rates. In order to enhance the amenities, a Social Club was built in 1985. Today this includes a lounge with stage and bar, as well as snooker and kitchen facilities. Current membership is over 1400. Outside there is the children's play area. The Social Club is adjacent to the Bowling Green, which serves a thriving Bowls Club.

Numerous sporting and recreational activities regularly take place within the Clubhouse. These include The Wyberton Over 60's Club and The Gardening Club. Other groups come from a wider area to use the facilities. Some of these being: The Motor Cycle Enthusiasts Club, The Deep Sea Fishermen, a Coarse Fishing Club and The Advanced Motorists.

Within the Sports and Social Club are a wide range of activities to cater for the diverse interests of the community.

Wyberton Colts 1966. Back row: Kevin Cocks, Keith Motley, Alan Louth, William Howarth, Barry Featherstone, Frazer Smith. Front row: Neil Johnson, Peter Vinter, Richard Melbourne, Mick Vinter, Ian Nimmo

Wyberton Road Names

London Road: Formerly the Turnpike Road. Called Kirton Road in the early 1700's, it was then known as Spalding Road until 1930. Ceased to be the A16 in 1989.

Low Road: Odforth Way until 1838. Probably called the Low road in contrast to the High road which would be the Turnpike Road.

Tytton Lane: Sometimes spelt Titton. Leading to the ancient hamlet of Titton on the site of the present Hall.

Slippery Gowt Lane: Gowt means an outfall or sluice. In this case the outfall of the Towns Drain into the Witham.

Closshill Lane: Known as Chossell Hill Lane.

Marsh Lane: Running from Slippery Gowt Lane towards Boston.

Heron Way: This name "appeared" almost overnight. It is the short section of Marsh Lane cut off when the new road from the Industrial estate to Slippery Gowt Lane was opened in 1998.

Silt Pit Lane: Known as Spring Pitts Lane. Called Silt Pit Lane in the 19th century because of the "silt pit" from which silt was extracted for road maintenance.

Green Lane: A name for a grassy lane without a hard stone surface. Used to be Holyday Hill Lane.

Bunkers Hill: Formerly Great Hill Lane in the 18th century.

Rowdyke: An old name. Runs alongside a field called Row- or Rawdykes in the 18th century.

Church Lane: The section by the Church was known as Church Way. Beyond Doubleroofed House it was called Wellslade Lane before 1930.

Birch Close: A small private housing cul-de-sac currently being completed off Low Road.

Causeway: This was called Church Lane until a causeway was laid in 1759 where there had previously been stepping stones.

Saundergate Lane: An old name. On some maps this was just called Saundergate. Saundergate Plott was one of the Medieval open fields.

Streetway: From Odforth Way to Rowting (or Routing) Cross this was a continuation of Saundergate. From there until the Sea bank it was called Streetway.

Wyberton Roads: Roads is an area of safe anchorage for ships waiting for a favourable tide.

Whileys Lane: Named after the Whiley family who lived in the cottage at the end of the lane. Formerly Axle-tree Hurn Field Lane.

Franks Lane: Formerly called Green Lane. Renamed in 1998 after Frank Johnson. Also known as Stepping Stone Way and Routing Cross Lane in the 18th century.

Whiley's cottage, Whileys Lane: Teddy Rushden with dog, Amos Garwell, Eli Whiley, Sam Dawson.

Southfields Lane: Now just a short grassy track but formerly a more important route connecting Wyberton and Frampton. Southfield was one of the original Medieval fields of the village.

Yarborough Road: Post War (1947) housing named after Mr. A. Cooke Yarborough, solicitor, who lived at the junction of Tytton Lane and Spalding Road. He was Chairman of the Parish Council from 1895 until his death in 1933.

Solway Avenue: Post War housing, about 1949, reputedly named by an R.D.C. official so that it was easy to read, write and remember!

Clarke Court: Housing Association dwellings built in the 1970's on land formerly owned by Mr. Bertie Clarke of Causeway House.

Tytton Court: A private development built in 1988 on the site of the farm buildings once belonging to Tytton Hall.

Saundergate Park: A small cul-de-sac off Saundergate Lane alongside Wyberton School, erected in the 1980's.

Cavendish Drive: A group of "Allison" homes built in 1968.

Parthian Avenue: Commenced in 1951. Houses and flats built by the Boston Rural District Council and named after a Submarine adopted by Boston during World War 2.

St. Leodegars Close: An extension of Parthian Avenue constructed in about 1972 and named after the Patron Saint of the village church.

Winter Way: Mainly flats and Old People's bungalows built in about 1970 and named after Wyberton Councillor, Mr. Joe Winter.

The Orchards: Elderly Persons' Units built by Boston Borough Council in 1982 on the site of a former orchard.

Granville Avenue: Built in 1934.

Solhem Avenue: Built in 1946. Timber houses of Swedish design. "Sol" and "hem" being Swedish names for Sun and Home.

Wyberton West Road: Once called Tiffin Browns Lane.

West End Road: Known as Westgate before the 18th century. The main drove road to the open fen.

Five House Lane: At least 300 years old. Sometimes Five Houses Lane.

Delfield Road: Development off the London Road by local builder, Mr. J. Dell. Commenced in the late 1950's.

Wybert Crescent: Named after the alleged Saxon earl who gave Wyberton its name.

Vine Crescent: Origin of name not known. Built in the 1960's.

Deldale Road: The road built in the 1970's connecting the Dellfield estate to Tytton Lane. The following roads lead off it:

Spice Avenue: Mr. H. Spice was a fruit grower who lived and farmed on Tytton Lane and was a Parish Councillor for over 40 years until he retired in 1946. A local benefactor.

Collingwood Crescent: Mr. Collingwood was a prominent figure in the 1950's and a churchwarden.

Tytton Close: A cul-de-sac off Deldale Road.

Bankside: Housing Association development built in 1978 along the bank of the Towns Drain.

Ralphs Lane: Formerly called Donington Road. Re-named after Ralph Smith, the last Wyberton man to be hung on a gibbet on that road, just over the Parish boundary.

Chain Bridge Road: Leading to the Chain Bridge, the bridge over the Hammond Beck and leading from the village to the Great Fen. (Not to be confused with the Wyberton High Bridge)

Old Hammond Beck Road: Running alongside the Old Hammond Beck, off West End Road.

Swineshead Road: Formerly the Turnpike Road leading westwards to Sleaford and Lincoln. Known as the Swineshead Ramper and called Sleaford Road in the 19th century.

New Hammond Beck Road: Running alongside the New Hammond Beck on the north side of the Swineshead Road.

Wortleys Lane: Named after the family owning and farming some of the land down the lane. Benjamin Wortley was a Parish Constable at the end of the 19th century.

Boardsides: Formerly an insignificant road running alongside the South Forty Foot Drain and the railway, fenced with high boarding in order that trains did not frighten the horses. It was part of the Great Fen Road.

Great Fen Road: By the Rugby Club. Leading to the Great Fen.

Westbridge Road: The new road opened in 1992 leading to Tesco and the new B&Q store.

A16: Opened in 1989 along the route of the former railway. The section through Wyberton has no special road name.

Joe Winter

Acknowledgements

The following have kindly allowed the reproduction of their photographs and documents:
Mary Abbott, Black Sluice Internal Drainage Board, Jim Blaylock, 8th Boston (Wyberton) Cub Scouts, Robert Bowser, Colin Brotherton, Terry Brown, Mary Cheer, Nellie Clarke, Cliff Clover, Joan Cocks, Joyce Colam, Stan Coupland, Chris Croxton, Colin Cullimore, Alan Dawson, Derek Falkinder, Barry Featherstone, Wally Franklin, Fred Galley, Jack Hall, Hazel Harrison, Brian Hayes, Hilary Healey, Ruby Hewson, Tim Higham, Phyllis Hill, Richard Ireson, Jim Jackson, David Leatherdale, Lincolnshire County Council, Ivy Louth, Stuart Lowther, J. Mastenbroek & Co., Ray Meads, Patrick Miller, Paul Mould, National Railway Museum, Aloyse Packe, David Perrin, Betty Pinder, Royal Society for the Protection of Birds, Brian Redman, Eileen Smith, Neil Smith, Eric Sutton, Maureen Thompson, Gwen Vaughan, Denis Walker, Colin Walter, Eve Warburton, John Watson, Eddie Welberry, Colin Welton, J. Winter.

The Wyberton History Group would also like to thank the many people who have provided information or given other assistance during the preparation of this book, in particular:
Richard Allday, Hazel Bond, Frank Carter, L. Clarke, Cliff Clover, Joyce Colam, Pat Cooke, Dorothy Cooper, E. Dring, Barbara Fletcher, B. Griffin, Mick Hammond, Hazel Harrison, Bill Hunt, G.O. Hutchinson, Jim Jackson, R. Jessop, Steven Membery, Martin Middlebrook, J. Morley, Emily Oelman, Aloyse Packe, Ray Robinson, Tilly Russell, M. Sansom, Richard Sharp, Colin Shepherdson, Hazel Smith, Helen Townsend, E. Welberry, W. Woods
and all the residents of Wyberton who are too numerous to mention individually.

Financial help was received from:
Awards for All, B&Q, The Borough of Boston

Any profits from the sale of this book are to be used for local charities

Wyberton History Group

Wyberton History Group. Back row: Colin Cullimore, Stephen Peel, Janet Parker, Alan Day, Alan Dawson, Colin Brotherton, June Barton, Jim Sharp, Bill Parker.
Seated: Stuart Lowther, Lilian Brabham, Richard Austin, Hilary Healey, Alison Austin.

Richard Ireson, Frank Bowser, Sally Bowser.   Artists: Glynn Williams, Margaret Cowe, Cyril Smith.   Photographer Denis Walker.   Guest writers: John and Elizabeth Watson.